Racism

Other books in the Current Controversies series:

Racism

Mary E. Williams, *Book Editor*

Daniel Leone, *President*
Bonnie Szumski, *Publisher*
Scott Barbour, *Managing Editor*
Helen Cothran, *Senior Editor*

CURRENT CONTROVERSIES

GREENHAVEN
PRESS®

THOMSON
™
GALE

San Diego • Detroit • New York • San Francisco • Cleveland
New Haven, Conn. • Waterville, Maine • London • Munich

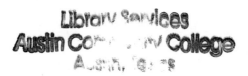

LIBRARY OF CONGRESS CATALOGING-IN-PUBLICATION DATA

Racism / Mary E. Williams, book editor.
   p. cm. — (Current controversies)
Includes bibliographical references and index.
ISBN 0-7377-1630-4 (pbk. : alk. paper) — ISBN 0-7377-1629-0 (lib. : alk. paper)
   1. Racism. 2. Racism—United States. 3. United States—Race relations.
I. Williams, Mary E., 1960– . II. Series.
HT1521.R3414 2004
305.8'00973—dc21   2003054020

Printed in the United States of America

Contents

Chapter 1: Is Racism a Serious Problem?

Yes: Racism Is Still a Serious Problem

No: Racism Is Declining

America. Much of the population will become racially and ethnically mixed, rendering the color divide obsolete. Class will replace race as a major source of social conflict.

Chapter 2: Is Racism Institutionalized in Society and Culture?

Yes: Institutionalized Racism Is Prevalent

No: Institutionalized Racism Is Not Prevalent

Chapter 3: Should Affirmative Action Be Abolished?

Yes: Affirmative Action Is Harmful

No: Affirmative Action Is Beneficial

same chances that whites have to attend college and enter professional fields. Eliminating it will do nothing to redress the systemic inequalities attached to race.

Chapter 4: How Can Racial Problems Be Resolved?

ity" group. Given these realities, Americans must expand their notions of race relations beyond black and white. Americans should educate themselves about race and form coalitions across ethnic lines to address continuing racial disparities.

Those who espouse racial "diversity" actually foster racism by spreading the notion that one's ethnic heritage determines one's thoughts and ideas. The only way to bring about racial integration is to absolutely disregard color while upholding the value of individualism and free will.

Social justice advocates should reexamine the philosophy of Martin Luther King Jr. and engage in the kind of nonviolent collective action he promoted as part of a global movement for human rights and dignity. Efforts to combat racism should be combined with a broader struggle against poverty, militarism, and consumerism.

Foreword

By definition, controversies are "discussions of questions in which opposing opinions clash" (Webster's Twentieth Century Dictionary Unabridged). Few would deny that controversies are a pervasive part of the human condition and exist on virtually every level of human enterprise. Controversies transpire between individuals and among groups, within nations and between nations. Controversies supply the grist necessary for progress by providing challenges and challengers to the status quo. They also create atmospheres where strife and warfare can flourish. A world without controversies would be a peaceful world; but it also would be, by and large, static and prosaic.

The Series' Purpose

The purpose of the Current Controversies series is to explore many of the social, political, and economic controversies dominating the national and international scenes today. Titles selected for inclusion in the series are highly focused and specific. For example, from the larger category of criminal justice, Current Controversies deals with specific topics such as police brutality, gun control, white collar crime, and others. The debates in Current Controversies also are presented in a useful, timeless fashion. Articles and book excerpts included in each title are selected if they contribute valuable, long-range ideas to the overall debate. And wherever possible, current information is enhanced with historical documents and other relevant materials. Thus, while individual titles are current in focus, every effort is made to ensure that they will not become quickly outdated. Books in the Current Controversies series will remain important resources for librarians, teachers, and students for many years.

In addition to keeping the titles focused and specific, great care is taken in the editorial format of each book in the series. Book introductions and chapter prefaces are offered to provide background material for readers. Chapters are organized around several key questions that are answered with diverse opinions representing all points on the political spectrum. Materials in each chapter include opinions in which authors clearly disagree as well as alternative opinions in which authors may agree on a broader issue but disagree on the possible solutions. In this way, the content of each volume in Current Controversies mirrors the mosaic of opinions encountered in society. Readers will quickly realize that there are many viable answers to these complex issues. By questioning each author's conclusions, students and casual readers can begin to develop the critical thinking skills so important to evaluating opinionated material.

Current Controversies is also ideal for controlled research. Each anthology in the series is composed of primary sources taken from a wide gamut of informational categories including periodicals, newspapers, books, United States and foreign government documents, and the publications of private and public organizations. Readers will find factual support for reports, debates, and research papers covering all areas of important issues. In addition, an annotated table of contents, an index, a book and periodical bibliography, and a list of organizations to contact are included in each book to expedite further research.

Perhaps more than ever before in history, people are confronted with diverse and contradictory information. During the Persian Gulf War, for example, the public was not only treated to minute-to-minute coverage of the war, it was also inundated with critiques of the coverage and countless analyses of the factors motivating U.S. involvement. Being able to sort through the plethora of opinions accompanying today's major issues, and to draw one's own conclusions, can be a complicated and frustrating struggle. It is the editors' hope that Current Controversies will help readers with this struggle.

Greenhaven Press anthologies primarily consist of previously published material taken from a variety of sources, including periodicals, books, scholarly journals, newspapers, government documents, and position papers from private and public organizations. These original sources are often edited for length and to ensure their accessibility for a young adult audience. The anthology editors also change the original titles of these works in order to clearly present the main thesis of each viewpoint and to explicitly indicate the opinion presented in the viewpoint. These alterations are made in consideration of both the reading and comprehension levels of a young adult audience. Every effort is made to ensure that Greenhaven Press accurately reflects the original intent of the authors included in this anthology.

Introduction

Nineteen sixty-three was a pivotal year in the history of race relations in the United States. In April of that year, Martin Luther King Jr. and several other civil rights leaders initiated a nonviolent protest campaign to desegregate public facilities in Birmingham, Alabama. City authorities turned fire hoses and police dogs on a large crowd of demonstrators—many of whom were children from local schools—and hundreds of protesters were beaten and arrested. The violent commotion was broadcast in national and world news media, allowing millions to witness the startling brutality of American racism for the first time. Two months later, President John F. Kennedy appeared on national television to proclaim his support for pending legislation that would forbid racial discrimination in employment, housing, and public accommodations. To help champion this legislation, civil rights advocates organized demonstrations in nearly every major city in the United States—culminating in a massive late-summer protest, the August 1963 March on Washington. Two hundred and fifty-thousand people—the largest protest group in U.S. history—marched to the Lincoln Memorial, where several civil rights leaders delivered speeches. The highlight of this event was Martin Luther King's eloquent and heartfelt "I Have a Dream" speech. "I have a dream," King yearned, "that my four little children will one day live in a nation where they will not be judged by the color of their skin but by the content of their character."

More than forty years later, King's words remain an emblem for those who aspire to create a society unimpeded by racism. Today's civil rights advocates, however, have stark differences of opinion over the interpretation of the slain leader's words and over the means by which his dream can be achieved. While progressives generally believe that King would support race-sensitive programs that attempt to counteract discrimination, such as affirmative action in education and employment, most conservatives argue that King would advocate colorblind policies in which character and merit—not race—determine hiring and college admissions decisions.

The concept of colorblindness—that is, public policy that is blind to race and ethnicity—is held in high regard by conservatives such as Ward Connerly and Glynn Custred. In the mid-1990s Connerly and Custred launched the California Civil Rights Initiative, a ballot measure designed to end affirmative action programs in hiring, contracting, and public education. Since the 1970s these programs had required California to ensure minority representation in its workforce and college populations by including race as a factor in its policy decisions. But in 1996 California voters adopted the new initiative, which declared that the state could not "discriminate against *or grant preferential treatment to* any individual or group on the basis of race, sex, color, ethnicity, or national origin in the operation of public employment, education, and contracting." The state of Washington passed a similar anti-affirmative action measure in 1998.

Supporters of the California and Washington initiatives maintain that such laws bring the United States closer to King's dream in which individuals are judged by their character and talents rather than by their race. They believe that affirmative action amounts to preferential treatment for minorities—a form of antiwhite "reverse discrimination" that thwarts the ideals of equal opportunity and fairness. In the opinion of Roger Clegg, general counsel of the Center for Equal Opportunity, "You can't undo the discrimination against some blacks by some whites in the past by requiring new discrimination on behalf of different blacks against different whites. The solution to the discrimination that exists is not more discrimination. It is to enforce the laws we have and to stop discriminating."

Another policy change that some conservatives believe would nurture King's dream and help bring racial discrimination to an end is to abandon the use of racial categories altogether. For one thing, the increase in the population of people of mixed ethnicity is quickly making the traditional "black/white/ Asian/Hispanic" categories obsolete, analysts point out. Moreover, many agree that race is mainly a social concept unrelated to an individual's personality or culture. This notion is supported by geneticists' explanations about differences in skin color, hair texture, or eye shape—surface traits that evolved over thousands of years as regional populations adapted to their environment. All humans belong to the same species, critics of racial categories assert, and they believe that abandoning the use of race as a signifier of identity would liberate people from the societal stereotypes, divisiveness, and self-fulfilling prophecies attached to race.

Supporting this call to abandon racial categories, Californian Ward Connerly proposed another measure, the Racial Privacy Initiative (RPI), which he believed would reinforce his state's 1996 law ending affirmative action and usher in an era of colorblindness. The intention of this initiative was to prohibit state agencies from classifying Californians by race, ethnicity, or national origin for any purpose having to do with public education, contracting, or employment. In effect, schools would not be allowed to report the racial make-up of their student bodies, government agencies could not recount what percentage of their workforce is minority, and no state policies could be made on the basis of race. In 2003, however, Californians voted against the passage of the RPI.

Despite this setback, Shelby Steele, a research fellow at Stanford University's Hoover Institution, believes that measures like the RPI would help correct the errors made by the 1960s civil rights establishment. Its major mistake, in Steele's opinion, was in deciding "to give resources and preferential treatment more to victims of racism than to people who simply suffer cultural and economic deprivations. . . . More and more racism was the lever one pushed to get entitlements and preferences, and cultural deprivation became more important as evidence of racism than as a problem to be overcome in its own right." Measures promoting colorblindness, however, would turn "a black fourth grader who can't read into simply a fourth grader who can't read." In other words, Steele argues, deprivation would no longer be seen as something attached to race, and the reading problem could be confronted head-on as an educational problem, not as a "racial" problem. As a result, educators could "get out the phonics books and teach reading, and forget about 'culturally specific learning styles,'" concludes Steele.

While conservatives hail anti-affirmative action measures and the potential abolishment of racial categories as signs of progress in the fight against discrimination, progressives often view these efforts as naive or—more troublingly—as disingenuous. "Indeed," writes University of Pennsylvania humanities professor Michael Eric Dyson, "conservatives in this country must be applauded for their perverse ingenuity in co-opting the legacy of Martin Luther King, Jr., and the rhetoric of the civil rights movement. . . . Many conservatives pretend to embrace a revolution that they, in fact, bitterly opposed." In Dyson's opinion, conservatives are attempting to appropriate the symbolism and moral authority of King to boost a political agenda that he actually would have resisted. Dyson maintains that conservatives are quoting King out of context when they point to his "I Have a Dream" speech as an implicit call to avoid race-sensitive policies. Examining the totality of King's life and work clarifies where he would have stood on affirmative action, Dyson points out. For example, in *Why We Can't Wait*, King wrote:

> No amount of gold could provide an adequate compensation for the exploitation and humiliation of the Negro in America down through the centuries. Not all the wealth of this affluent society could meet the bill. Yet a price can be placed on unpaid wages. The ancient common law has always provided a remedy for the appropriation of the labor of one human being by another. This law should be made to apply for American Negroes. The payment should be in the form of a massive program by the government of special, compensatory measures which could be regarded as a settlement in accordance with the accepted practice of common law.

While Martin Luther King Jr. certainly dreamed of a society unfettered by race, he envisioned it happening only *after* oppression and racism were destroyed, Dyson argues. Dismantling racism, in King's view, would require policies that place minorities at an advantage to make up for the lack of opportunities they had endured for centuries.

Law professor Paul Butler agrees, and argues further that calls for colorblindness in contemporary America are irresponsible and counterproductive. "You can't have three hundred years of law and public policy all designed to subordinate a group—to be actively hostile to them—and then say, 'Hey, everything's hunky-dory. Now we're going to be color-blind. Pull yourself up by your own bootstraps.'" While Butler agrees that race is a social concept, it is a concept that has created social realities, such as racial discrimination, that cannot be instantly debunked at will. In his opinion, advocates for colorblindness "pretend, like all of a sudden, after race existed with a vengeance for three hundred years, that now it doesn't exist anymore." He insists that facing reality requires policy makers to "see human beings as human including their race. We won't be seeing human beings—we won't be truly seeing—if we're partially blind. That's the irony of the color-blind debate. How can we see if we're blind?"

Echoing Butler's sentiments, most mainstream civil rights organizations do not support the abolishment of racial categories. For example, the National Association for the Advancement of Colored People (NAACP) maintains that racial data collection provides the tools necessary to identify institutional bias when it occurs. Racial statistics help to uncover patterns of discrimination in housing, employment, law enforcement, and health care—necessary information if authorities are to enforce antidiscrimination laws, NAACP analysts point out. Moreover, America would not be able to track its progress in conquering racial discrimination without reliable information about the opportunities that are available to different racial groups. Suppression of such information by banning the use of racial categories, argues former Justice Department attorney Alan Jenkins, amounts to censorship: "It bears noting that facts belong to no one group or agenda, to no ideology or political party. . . . Information and the liberty to use it . . . are hallmarks of a free society. Efforts to suppress [racial] information gathering are threats not merely to the political left or right, but to the truth."

In the year after Martin Luther King delivered his "Dream" speech, Congress passed the Civil Rights Law of 1964, which prohibited discrimination in hiring, housing, and public accommodations because of race, color, religion, sex, or national origin. In the twenty-first century, however, analysts and policy makers remain divided over how the civil rights vision can best be advanced. *Racism: Current Controversies* offers a variety of perspectives on the status of civil rights and race relations, and provides different views on how to eradicate racism and its legacies.

Chapter 1

Is Racism a Serious Problem?

Chapter Preface

"I was in a popular drugstore looking for a hair product," writes black writer Robin Yaesha Deane in a March 18, 2000, *Los Angeles Times* editorial. "Surprisingly, it was not in aisle 4 with the other hair products. It was in the front of the store, locked up in a glass cabinet with a bolt lock. The hair colors and perms kits for African American women were the only products locked and marked 'ethnic products' even though Los Angeles is a city where there is a diversity of ethnicities. The items were locked because management feared that these items would be stolen if unlocked."

Many blacks, Latinos, and Asians report experiences similar to Deane's: disrespectful treatment, poor service, prejudiced comments, and encounters with people who are suspicious of them because of their ethnicity or color. While civil rights laws passed in the 1960s forbid blatant racial discrimination in employment, housing, and public facilities, attitudes about minorities have been slower to change, analysts report. Nonwhites may no longer have to face "whites only" signs legally barring them from public accommodations, but more subtle forms of bias—from ethnic stereotypes to hidden doubts about minorities' intelligence—remain prevalent, many commentators maintain. Part of the reason such bias persists, they point out, is because social segregation still exists in most American communities. As a result, people of different races generally have few opportunities to form friendships or to interact with each other in meaningful ways. In Deane's words, "White Americans are afraid of us [blacks] because they don't know us. . . . They don't know we have assets, inventions, investments and we do more than hip-hop, dunk, rap and commit crimes." In addition, many analysts believe that negative stereotypes have a cumulative effect, resulting in a form of societal discrimination that creates and maintains educational and economic disparities between whites and minorities.

Other analysts, although they grant that racism still exists, claim that it is definitely on the decline. Experiences such as the drugstore incident described by Deane should be seen in perspective, they argue—that is, with the recognition that race relations may be flawed but are nevertheless progressing. Many surveys suggest that white attitudes toward minorities underwent great changes in the twentieth century. For example, one study shows that in 1933, 75 percent of whites perceived blacks as inherently lazy—but by 1993, only 5 percent of whites would make such a claim. Another mid-1990s survey revealed that 90 percent of whites would vote for a qualified black presidential candidate; in the 1950s, almost no whites would support a black candidate. Even entrenched patterns of social segregation are breaking down, as evidenced by the increase in interracial neighborhoods, relationships, and marriages, observers point out. In time, argues black businessman Ward Connerly, Americans will "merge and melt into each other." Connerly believes that this melding is a long-term process that deserves recognition: "Throughout our history, there has been a constant intermingling of people—even during the long apartheid of segregation and Jim Crow. It is malicious as well as unreasonable not to acknowledge that in our own time the conditions for anger have diminished and the conditions for connection have improved."

As the opinions of Robin Yaesha Deane and Ward Connerly reveal, views on the seriousness of racism and racial discrimination vary widely. The following chapter presents different perspectives on the unsettled issue of whether racism remains prevalent in America.

Racism Still Exists

by Halford H. Fairchild

About the author: *Halford H. Fairchild is a professor of psychology and black studies at Pitzer College in Claremont, California.*

There are those who assert that racism is obsolete and not a contemporary problem. But racism is a current event; only its expression is more disguised and subtle. And it requires intervention.

We can best understand the contemporary reality of racism by delving into its past. In antiquity, knowledge of racial differentiation was not necessarily accompanied by dehumanizing sentiments; indeed, the ancient Greeks and Romans looked upon the ancient Ethiopians with respect and romanticism. The ancient Egyptians' awareness of racial variation did not carry with it the dehumanization of those who were superficially different.

The Development of Racism

The idea of race took on the patina of a scientific enterprise primarily in the early to mid-1800s, as part of what is largely known as the European Enlightenment. Scientists at that time, particularly in biology and botany, were earnest in classifying the diversity of life on Earth, and part of this classification included the human species. Perhaps because of ethnocentrism and cultural chauvinism, the classification of human beings included a rank ordering with Europeans at the top of the scale and Africans at the bottom.

The institutionalization of slavery within the Americas required an intellectual justification for the mistreatment of millions of African men, women and children. Muslims had mirrored this process of intellectually justifying enslavement in the earlier enslavement of East Africans. Slavery required racism and was the proximate cause of it.

Racism became unique in the United States largely because of the efforts to abolish slavery. These efforts intensified the efforts of slavery's apologists to justify their "peculiar institution." Thus if we can say that contemporary racism is a product of American slavery, then we must also accept the premise that

American slavery demonstrates other consequences that are as alive and well today as is racism.

Aversive Racism

Racism in contemporary world affairs is disguised, and it is what some refer to as symbolic racism, modern racism or aversive racism. These eschew the old-fashioned, redneck ideology of white supremacy and black inferiority and instead espouse support for the ideals of equality in human affairs. Yet these ideals of equality are discordant with the preference for the status quo of white privilege.

Thus aversive racism is manifested in opposition to programs and policies that seek to undo white privilege or provide advantages to blacks on the basis of historical discrimination.

> *"Racism is a current event; only its expression is more disguised and subtle."*

Interestingly, contemporary research in social psychology demonstrates that the aversive racist is unaware of his or her racism; much of contemporary racism is an unconscious process.

In a series of interesting experiments, some in the laboratory and some in real-world settings, social psychologists have illustrated the presence of unconscious or aversive racism in a number of contexts. The effects of aversive racism are manifold and affect the quality of life of Africans and African Americans both physically and psychologically. Thus we see the ravages of racism at work in the appalling statistics of HIV/AIDS in Africa and among African Americans. We see the life-and-death consequences of old-fashioned and modern racism in the rates of infant mortality among Africans and African Americans as well as their much higher rates of preventable deaths from hypertension, heart disease, cancer and violence.

The current effects of racism have led to a widening of the economic gulf between white Americans and black Americans. Although the proportions of African Americans in the middle and upper classes have increased, so too has the proportion of African American children reared in poverty. The presence of African Americans in the higher echelons of corporate America, government and the military is about one-tenth of what one would expect given a system of true equal opportunity.

To solve these problems of structured inequality, we must first acknowledge the reality of racism in contemporary world affairs. We can no longer afford to hide from this reality. We must make conscious unconscious racism. Then we must develop and propagate social and institutional norms and values that reject racism—conscious and unconscious—and advance true equal opportunity.

Blacks Are Burdened by Stereotypes

by Marcia Cantarella

About the author: *Marcia Cantarella is an assistant dean at Princeton University.*

Editor's Note: This selection was originally delivered as a speech to the Fourth Universalist Society at the Fourth Universalist Church in New York, New York, on February 13, 2001.

In 1969 when my father, Whitney Young, wrote the book *Beyond Racism* Blacks in America had cause for optimism. We had seen passed some of the most historic civil rights legislation since the 14th Amendment nearly a hundred years earlier. Civil rights acts guaranteed voting rights, non-discrimination in housing, public accommodations and employment. Black was beautiful. Our leaders, including my father, graced the covers of *Time* and *Newsweek*. Even our urban rage, destructive though it was, reflected a self-affirming anger. We were mad as hell and not going to take it anymore. No more shuffling obsequies. Through an agenda that became known as "Affirmative Action," there was an institutional effort to redress the impact of past race-based discrimination by taking affirmative steps to include Blacks and others in hiring, purchasing goods and education. We were poised, damn it all, to get "Beyond Racism."

And as most black folks lived at the margins of American life, the reality was we had to get beyond racism if we were to have any hope at all. In Richard Wright's tremendous novel *Native Son*, the protagonist Bigger Thomas living in a white household sees all that he has not had—the house, the clothes, the fun. By the 1960's, the media had made apparent to all Blacks the difference between their quality of life and that of the Cleaver's or Dick Van Dyke's.

In 1967, the median income for Whites was $8,300 and for Blacks only $4,900—59% of White income and less than half what the government said was needed to live in the urban areas where Blacks were dominant.

While we made up 10% of the population, we were 36% of the impoverished. When he wrote in 1969, the unemployment rate was, like today, 4%, but for urban Blacks it was 20%. And Blacks were paid 36–42% less for the same jobs as Whites. This remained true even with a college education.

Where Blacks Stand Today

And so now here we are 30 years after my father's death. Where do we stand according to the National Urban League's *State of Black America 2000*? While our unemployment rate has gone down for Black Americans, it is still twice as high as White Americans' regardless of the level of educational achievement. We are still twice as likely to live in poverty. Yet there has been progress. Not only are more of us attending colleges and professional schools, thanks to affirmative efforts, but as William Bowen and Derek Bok have pointed out in their ground breaking book, *The Shape of the River*, the impact of that effort has been significant. They document a real premium in both the wages and the levels of satisfaction of those Black students who have been enabled to attend highly selective colleges. The wage gap is less, the civic participation rate higher.

"[The Black] unemployment rate . . . is still twice as high as White Americans' regardless of the level of educational achievement."

And so progress has been made. And yet we are clearly not "Beyond Racism." A Black man can even now be dragged behind a truck to his death, stopped in New Jersey while driving because he's Black, or have a greater chance of being on death row than in college. While talking to my son, Mark, recently who just bought a home in a White suburb of Boston, he reflected that while shoveling snow from the driveway, he wondered if anyone realized that he was the homeowner and not the handyman. Growing up in an affluent section of NYC [New York City] he could not get cabs or was followed when visiting his dad in the executive offices at Bloomingdales. Like him, I know that unless I am wearing a suit, I am likely to be taken for a maid in our apartment building. I have heard students over and over, both at NYU [New York University] and at Princeton, describe the annoyance of being expected to "represent" the race in the classroom where they may be the sole brown face. While biracial marriages increase, the children they produce often find that they must deal with the fact that some part of their identity is less acceptable than the other part. What kind of sense does that make?

Harmful Stereotypes

These examples are all the product of racial stereotyping. Unlike White folks, Blacks are somehow expected to be a monolithic, homogeneous people whose characteristics are skewed to the negative. By what reason are we expected to represent such unity when, thanks to miscegenation, forced or voluntary, we share the blood of the French (as in Creole), Scots, British, and every other type who owned slaves—as well as Native Americans and Hispanics. The range of skin colors in the Black population is as rich and nuanced us any palette on earth. And equally rich and nuanced is our range of experiences. In the 19th century you could find us as cooks and cowboys, idlers and intellectuals, poets and plowmen, soldiers and seamstresses, educators and entrepreneurs. And time has only widened the possibilities. We can be computer makers and cabinet members, deans and dentists, attorneys and astronauts. Given the dazzling array of the spectrum of identities represented by Black folks, stereotypes do not sit well with us. I believe that stereotyping is especially grating in America given our national mythology.

> *"Unlike White folks, Blacks are somehow expected to be a monolithic, homogeneous people whose characteristics are skewed to the negative."*

Americans believe strongly in individualism and individual freedom. That is the underpinning of the Bill of Rights. Our heroes of fictional fame are all quirky, rugged individualists from James Fennimore Cooper's Leatherstocking to every character ever played by [Humphrey] Bogart or [Spencer] Tracy or [John] Wayne. While we have been characterized as a nation of sheep and are the home of the mass market, our philosophical origins tilt to the factions of [James] Madison's "Federalist 10," [Ralph Waldo] Emerson's "Self-Reliance" and Ayn Rand's *Atlas Shrugged*. While we need community, we still revel in our individuality. Blacks, immersed in this culture from its very beginnings, are no different. Are John Shaft and Sam Spade very different anti-heroes? Over the past ten years, we have seen more mass marketing give way to niche marketing as technology has made targeting and personalization more possible. If the majority of Americans do not want to be lumped together, Blacks do not either. Stereotyping creates dissonance and discomfort.

One of the most damaging of stereotypes is the one that assumes that Blacks lack ambition and have no aspirations. Again the notion of socio-economic mobility in America was documented as far back as [political philosopher Alexis de] Tocqueville's writings in the 1830's. The brilliant contemporary chronicler of American life, Studs Terkel, studied aspiration in his book *American Dreams: Lost and Found*. What is clear is that in every one of his hundreds of interviews, everyone has a dream, each dream is unique, and the poignancy comes through in the presence or absence of hope. Journalist and NYU professor, David Dent, engaged in a singular exploration exclusively among Black folks. And there resonated again the dreams of "moving on up," "getting a piece of the pie," to lift from the old *Jefferson's* TV show's theme song. In America, the urge to move up (in status) has become connected to the need for wealth or at the very least celebrity. The tragedy of *Death of a Salesman* was Willie Loman's spiraling down in prestige as his earning power diminished.

Blacks have watched as wave after wave of immigrants has entered America in search of the ability to be self-sufficient, personally free and upwardly mobile. And wave after wave of immigrants—the Irish, the Italians, Jews and now Asians have achieved these goals. They have moved on from the ghettos of the Lower East Side and moved up to the Upper East Side (or here to the even more chichi West Side!). And a great many Black folks have also. Yet in the many minds who stereotype us we have never left Harlem. My son can't get a cab because the driver assumes that he lives in Harlem. When I leave my apartment I must be going home to Harlem. Yet let me list for you the Black millionaires that I know: Vernon Jordan, partner at Lazard Freires, Dick Parsons, COO of Time Warner, Ed Lewis, publisher of *Essence*, and Earl Graves, publisher of *Black Enterprise*. Then there is Ken Chenault, new CEO of American Express, or Frederick Raines of Fortune 500 Fannie Mae Corp., or Thomas Jones of Citibank.

Unseen People

My childhood in Atlanta in the 1950's was spent in a segregated environment where we could not swim in public pools or play on public tennis courts. So my friends' parents built their own pools and tennis courts. There has been wealth and status and persons of fine educational pedigree throughout our history here. But those are not the dominant media images. Thank God for Bill Cosby. The Huxtable family was more familiar to me than any I have seen on FOX TV which perpetrates cultural myths of ignorance and buffoonery as the Black status quo.

Once these negative images begin to dominate in the minds of employers and teachers and bureaucrats, how is it possible for Blacks to be viewed as unique individuals filled with aspirations and desires? Our true selves are as unseen as [Ralph] Ellison's characterization of the Invisible Man.[1] My taste in music runs to romantic ballads and not rap. I can enjoy equally Gordon Parks or Picasso, [Georges] Brague or [Romare] Beardon, ribs or risotto. But going through your minds is the thought "but you are an exception." Let me describe a few students I have come to know over the past twelve years, Black students of different backgrounds. There is the chemistry student pursuing his doctorate at [the University of Pennsylvania], who is fluent in Chinese, and the comparative literature major with masters degrees from Columbia and Oxford who is now an executive at Morgan Stanley. Her sister is a doctor, her mother was a domestic and a caterer. There was the young social worker who loves professional wrestling, the history major who aspires to sports management, the engineer from Ohio who was a Princeton Rhodes finalist, the engineer now at Wharton who filed several patents at Lockheed before he was 25. There was the student from Nashville who won a grant to study the acoustics of St. Marks in Venice and went on to become a computer consultant at Anderson. I can go on and on.

---

1. Ellison's 1947 novel *Invisible Man* tells the story of a black man who is "invisible" to American society because of his race.

They are each uniquely gifted, hard-workers and have their own aspirations. What is painful to observe, however, is the extra burden they carry.

Tisha's Story

Let me outline a couple of scenarios that may demonstate what I mean by burdens. A student, whom we will call Tisha, has gone to a good public school in Queens. She has done exceedingly well and been a leader in a variety of organizations. She is encouraged by her teachers to apply to college—to good colleges. Her parents have worked hard to make a comfortable living. Tisha is the oldest and so will be the first in the family to attend college. It is their dream that she will become a doctor and have wealth, prestige and stability. She had done well in her high school biology and chemistry, classes, she was kind. They thought she would be a fine doctor. When Tisha filled in her college applications, where it asked possible majors she wrote "biology," and under career goals, she wrote "medicine." Her family proudly told everyone at church that Tisha was going to college to become a doctor. She had become, for her community, the embodiment of the American dream. Once at college many things happened. She took the math placement test and was placed in an entry-level class as her high school had not offered calculus. However, since she had not had calculus, she could not take, as a freshman, the chemistry classes needed for pre-med students. Those would have to wait. So she

> **"If the majority of Americans do not want to be lumped together, Blacks do not either."**

wisely took other courses which were required. She discovered that she loved her anthropology class. While she struggled with math and a biology class much harder than [the one in] high school, she was getting A's in anthropology and literature. As educators, we hope students will have these experiences where they sort out their strengths, weaknesses and interests. However, Tisha began to panic. Her family and community wanted, needed, her to be a doctor and she was not doing well in math and science. When her parents came for parents' weekend she said that all was well. She could not disappoint them. She was becoming depressed by her sense of failure. Her White roommate, whose parents and even grandparents were college educated, did not understand. So Tisha kept her sadness to herself. Anyway, she did not want to look dumb. People might think she had only gotten in because she was Black and not because she was qualified. In fact, she was beginning to wonder herself with the low math and science grades, if she had indeed been an "affirmative action" selection. So she kept her doubts and fears to herself. She stopped going to meals and gradually came down with the flu. As a result of being ill, her grades in the classes she loved began to suffer. Despite flyers and announcements about support groups, tutors, and counselors, she was afraid to reveal her insecurities because she did not want others to think that she was dumb because she was

Black. In her sophomore year she happened to take another anthropology class from a young African American professor. In the professor she saw something she wanted to be. This was a woman, with a doctorate, who looked like her— even had tiny braids. Tisha began to open up with this professor and revealed that ever since she had tutored in high school she had wanted to teach. Anthropology had captured her imagination. She wanted to major in it—but how to tell her parents, her community, that she would not be a doctor. She would be a disappointment. Her professor suggested that the Dean speak to Tisha's parents. By her junior year Tisha had begun again to be involved in campus groups. Once she dropped the pre-med classes, her grades took off as she reveled in this field she had never heard of. This is not at all an uncommon scenario. With the weight of the world on their shoulders, Black students struggle through and persist in challenging courses of study that White kids would drop without a care. Tisha found a Black mentor in her department. However, with only 1200 Black Ph.D.'s graduated annually, those role models and mentors are scarce. Depression, isolation, anger and frustration are the emotions which accompany far too many Tisha's on their paths.

Malcolm's Story

But what of the affluent, the middle-class Black youth? Consider a young man named Malcolm. His parents were both attorneys who had met at Yale Law School. They lived in Scarsdale. Malcolm had gone to a superb public school where most of his friends were White. Most of his parents' friends, associates, and neighbors were White. That was the world that he knew. He played tennis and lacrosse. He wore Ralph Lauren and John Weitz ties. He thought he might go to law school or business school. When he got to college his roommate's mother asked what his SAT scores had been, as if to challenge his ability and his right to be there, as if he were somehow not as good as her son who, being White, had gotten in "legitimately." He was angry but said nothing. In classes he found himself expected to comment on issues of inner city Blacks though he had grown up in an upscale suburb. He became angrier. He played lacrosse and, since not many Black students did, most of his alliances were with White students. He began to be criticized by other Black

> *"One of the most damaging of stereotypes is the one that assumes that Blacks lack ambition and have no aspirations."*

students for not hanging out with them. That made him angry. As these angers, all internalized, built up he began to drink more, making it harder to get up in the morning and to make early classes. His grades began to slide. Fortunately an upperclassman spotted what was happening and urged him to talk, and not to internalize his angers, but to give them constructive voice. Ultimately, and with the help of his parents who had themselves lived this experience, he came to understand that the problem was not with him, but with others who were limited in their visions of what he could be.

For both of these students there was pressure to achieve. It is virtually an axiom of the "American Dream" that each generation will do better than the one before. However, because these students were being perceived as less than others, inherently less than others, their sense of pressure to achieve was more powerful, painful and poignant. To ask for help, to complain of ill treatment was in their minds to affirm what seemed to be thought of them. However, the impact was to create a self-fulfilling prophecy. Both students began acting out in depression, in self-doubt and in anger. They turned on themselves making the victimized the victim. Recent studies show a performance gap between Black and White students in college. We believe that the gap can be attributed directly to the two scenarios I have described. In addition there is evidence that financial pressures, especially the weight of student loans that must be borne by the majority of Black students of the lower middle class (kept there by ongoing wage discrimination) contribute significantly to the attrition of Black students. They often carry more hours of work at school and cannot afford enriching summer experiences. I am proud to say that my institution, Princeton, has just taken the lead in eliminating student loans to further increase our socioeconomic and ethnic diversity.

> *"So long as the rich array of who we [Blacks] are, in all our colors and experiences, dreams and talents, is not recognized, then we will not get beyond racism."*

Growing Beyond Racism

And so racial stereotyping itself engenders conditions which perpetrate the situations that perpetuate the stereotypes. When people who are set up to fail do so, they are then called failures, and when they don't, they must be exceptional. But the reality is that most Blacks are exceptional by that standard. Though set up to fail, most don't. The media, however, . . . represents the extremes of the spectrum. We must be Cosby or crooks. The vast majority of upwardly striving, hard-working, honest, good Black folks are not newsworthy. And so as long as the rich array of who we are, in all our colors and experiences, dreams and talents, is not recognized, then we will not get beyond racism. The individuality that is so much at the heart of the American ethos must be accorded to Blacks as well. You, each of us, must challenge away first impressions and seek to know us as individuals. We must engage in common cause and come to some degree of mutual respect. And I do mean mutual respect because we have learned through your distrust of our abilities, to distrust your sincerity. Let your actions prove us wrong. Let a first action be to let the media know that they must seek to represent Blacks in breadth. Study yourselves the privileges of

Whiteness. Don't take them for granted. They are true. Getting beyond racism means conscious affirmation of the worth and total uniqueness of each individual. It is a position consistent with our claim for the sanctity of human life. We cannot claim certain principles and then apply them selectively. Life, liberty and the pursuit of happiness for me and mine, not you and yours. Liberty and justice for me but not for you. In all our wars, Blacks have fought to preserve those principles for all of us, only to have them consistently denied to many if not most of us. Operating by stereotype we function in a state of imperfect knowledge. The only person we can stand in judgement of, or know well, is ourselves. Operating from a willingness to learn from and value everyone we encounter, we can grow beyond racism.

Social Segregation Persists

by Sarah E. Hinlicky

About the author: *Sarah E. Hinlicky is a student at Princeton Theological Seminary.*

The cardinal rule of writing about race is: don't. There are several reasons why. First, it is impossible to say anything new. Second, it axiomatically follows that it is impossible to say anything interesting. Third, it is impossible to avoid offense; or, in laboring to avoid offense, whatever humble point that may have been trying to assert itself will be buried under piles of apologies, qualifications, and assurances of the goodwill of the author. Rather than submit oneself to such circuitous torture, the wise writer observes the rules and politely declines to write about race.

Anyone even marginally curious about the issue is forced to wonder how the American dialogue about race has ground to such a halt. Schools of thought on racial issues proliferate, yet they find no room for discussion, worse yet no point to discussion, among them. The unsurprising outcome of this refusal to discuss is that race is simply ignored, forgotten, and extracted from our collective American life altogether. Even the *New York Times* hardly ever mentions it except to demonize [former] Mayor Rudolph Giuliani's police. Race relations no longer command public attention. In thirty short years we went from a national rally around a man with a dream to . . . nothing. In our eminently pragmatic America, lip service to equality in the dubious form of affirmative action has become the main focus of what little discussion remains.

By now I've already trespassed the cardinal rule against writing about race, so I have nothing to lose by writing a little more. Perhaps an examination of the social interactions between ordinary blacks and whites can shed some light on how we've reached this impasse. Acknowledging the impossibility of newness, I offer the following tale precisely for its sheer unremarkableness, the typical college experience common to nice young white Americans raised in monochrome neighborhoods.

Cafeteria Segregation

I went to a small, private, liberal arts college in the South. The school's location didn't make it especially prone to racism, contrary to my expectations as a snooty Yankee. I can't recall any racial incidents on campus during my four-year tenure there. The white folks I knew were like me, conscientiously trying to be color-blind and sensitive to minority concerns. A couple were very outspoken about the imperative of racial justice. These, strangely, were the only ones I ever heard indulge in racial slurs. I suppose they considered themselves safe on account of their highly public convictions, as if their truthful claim to know "a lot of blacks" somehow made it okay to slam them. But even that was rare. Civil rights babies all, we knew the right side of history and were sticking to it.

Funny thing is, my racial enlightenment, and that of all my white friends, didn't make a smidgen of difference. Our school was segregated anyway. Not legally, but voluntarily, and enforced by social strictures more binding than anything government could impose. Take a look around the cafeteria, for instance. There's a sea of pink and peach faces, maybe one or two truly white from hangovers, all gathered around the front tables by the salad bar. Look farther back and at the other end of the room, by the cereal and the back door, all the brown and black faces together. It's embarrassing, like Rosa Parks on the bus, except the other way around: we don't care to sit in the front with you, thanks, we'll retreat to the back on our own. The rare breaches of the invisible wall between us happened only after baseball or football practices, when the players all sat together, an integration based on camaraderie and, I guess, sweat.

For ordinary whites, though, the wall remained insurmountable. I would imagine trying to strike up a conversation as, in my mind's eye, I meander towards the black students. I try to look completely natural. Instead, I look silly. My motivation to chat with these people, who to my eyes have only their color in common, can only be some peculiar manifestation of my white conscience. Maybe I am curious about "black culture," or maybe I feel it is my postmodern prerogative to engage the other purely on account of the other's otherness, or maybe I feel guilty that I always sit in the front and they always sit in the back.

Silly. I also look scared. Who am I to presume on their territory? What do I have to say that could possibly interest them, when I don't even know what about them constitutes "them"? I am at a total loss as to what attitude won't be viewed with immediate sus-

> *"[Blacks and whites] have simply remained apart. Albeit nonviolently . . . color still divides us."*

picion. But that's just it. In fact, there is no correct attitude, because the situation itself is unnatural to the point of impossibility. Our segregation means that I am always a person of one color approaching a person of another color, with the absolute arbitrariness of color defining the whole interaction. It doesn't get any more unnatural than that. So I give in, my better (are they better?) intentions defeated, and I sit back down at my seat, up in the front.

Neutral Territory

It wasn't always, if I may say it, as black and white as that. I did know a few black students at college—a very few. The key thing was to find some common ground. Despite the language barrier, it was reasonably easy to meet the deaf black students within the large deaf community at my alma mater because their primary label was deaf, not black. Likewise in the theater we were thespians first, so the stage became neutral territory. I think of an astonishingly gifted young black man who starred in a number of our shows. He was widely adored for his talent, his humor, his style, his affectionate nature coupled with a breathtaking intensity, and, yes, his skin. I doubt he ever knew what a sheer relief it was for us to be with him, some living contact with a slice of enigmatically familiar America, the genuine article, of which we were normally deprived. He was like a little window through which we peeked at a hidden segment of our nation, normally revealed to us only by TV, and there superficially. At the same time and in a perverse way, our friendship with him was a safety net. He was our excuse to chime in with the ubiquitous "I can't be a racist—I have black friends." I wonder how many times white Americans have hauled out that phrase against the accusations coming not only from others, but from within themselves as well.

> *"Color . . . happens to make the cultural segregation all the more obvious."*

Another neutral territory encounter took place in the Writing Center, where I worked under the gentle title of "peer consultant." One afternoon a black freshman in English 131 came in for some advice on the documentation of his research paper. His explanation of the topic, black fraternities, distracted me entirely from the matter at hand. Honestly, I was horrified. He told me with evident satisfaction about the brutal initiation rites and absolute allegiance to the group required to become a brother. One practice involved blindfolding the pledges, driving them to and depositing them in a small town several hundred miles away, stripping them of jackets, money, and phone cards, and then expecting them to make it home safely. "It's to teach us," he said, "about not being allowed to travel in public, about having to hide out from the Klan. It teaches us strength, endurance, self-reliance." "It's not like that anymore," I commented. "It's our heritage," he replied. "We are brothers. We must be linked together by a common bond." The common bond, I realized with a chill, is a history of abuse from people of my color.

Then he added that, as far as he knew, most black fraternities were in legal trouble for hazing, which he took to be a sign of further white oppression of the black brotherhood. Who needs white oppression, I thought, when you so effectively oppress your own? Perhaps this young man also thought it oppression that most of the white students on campus were opposed to the introduction of black fraternities. The reason was simple: the group pressure would prevent any black student from ever again joining a "white" fraternity and the inevitable segregation would deepen, institutionalized all over again.

What all this means is that we—by which I mean America's newest grown-ups of European descent—were raised by a system that did and didn't work. It did work because the very idea of judging someone on the basis of skin color is, I would assert, anathema to the vast majority of white twenty- and thirty-somethings in this country. It

> *"Black America and white America are different cultures, and these cultures still distrust one another."*

didn't work because, despite our equitable attitude towards blacks, our convictions have languished in the abstract. We have simply remained apart. Albeit nonviolently (an important qualification), color still divides us.

Color or Culture?

Or is it really color? I wonder. I've detected little hints that it isn't color at all. There's a girl I knew, for instance, who became black. I thought it was a stretch for this blonde-haired, blue-eyed young woman, but she pulled it off with what seemed remarkable ease. The first sign of her transformation was that she started to date only black men, strongly encouraging me to do the same. (I thought it made no more sense to date a man solely because he was black than it did to refuse to date a man solely because he was black.) Then it was her music—suddenly all she listened to was rap, hip-hop, R&B, and sometimes a little soul. Her slang vocabulary evolved, followed by a subtly altered accent, and soon she had become our local expert on all things African American. She, the white-skinned, accepted them, the black-skinned, and they accepted her too without any apparent trouble, and along the way she also accepted a new identity—a black one, despite her skin color. I thought it odd—not objectionable, just odd—but then again, I guess she never had much of an identity at all as one among many of the great whitewashed masses. Now she does.

Another little hint is the racial assortment of the church I attended for a while. Some of the members had black skin. Almost none of those, however, were African Americans, but rather Africans who have become Americans recently. In other words, immigrants, not the descendants of slaves. It's not that the latter wouldn't have been welcome in our church—quite the contrary—but they rarely came. The immigrants, though, are just like any other immigrants melting into American society, and their color was not a point of much interest.

No, I think it's culture. Color's role now is to demarcate conveniently the change in culture, and it happens to make the cultural segregation all the more obvious. Think about it: no one is terribly concerned about whether or not the Koreans or the Peruvians are mingling adequately with whites. Of course they are, because that's the culture they're joining, that of the immigrants who believed that new and better opportunities awaited them. My forebears, for instance, came here in freedom, or at least some kind of it. Whether they were plagued by poverty or persecution, war or imminent war, they set sail for America in full confidence that freedom awaited them on the other side of the Atlantic, in exotic-sounding places like . . . Nebraska. And once here, they could shed their pasts, their accents, and their cooking in one swift generation's time, blending into the free American masses with only a surname, at most, to betray their roots.

Not so with our black brethren who were brought to these shores in chains. America was not a courageous choice. Beautiful freedom was not a guarantee. It was something withheld, bequeathed, squelched, earned, desired, demanded, but never just plain assumed. To this day, regardless of fair treatment or mistreatment, the heavy history of enslavement hangs over black Americans, like [author] Toni Morrison's [character] Beloved who haunts the barely free Sethe. They can't help but collectively embody a reproach to the American dream, whether they want to or not. The cultural identity created by that status can't be shrugged off lightly, like my great-grandmother's recipe for sauerkraut. For those bearing the black color, participation in broad, i.e., "white," American culture must remain an ambiguous option. And white Americans in turn can't help but recall that the origin of a different black culture is past injustice by whites. Maybe not by any one of us particularly or by our forebears either, but regardless of what we think about those past perpetrators of injustice, we still share their skin color.

Black America and white America are different cultures, and these cultures still distrust one another. Moving across color lines means also moving across culture lines. It's easy enough to learn to be colorblind. Is it possible to become culture-blind? Maybe there's an answer to be found, but I think I'd better quit now, since I'm not supposed to be writing about race in the first place.

White Supremacist Influence Is Increasing

by Peter L. DeGroote

About the author: *Peter L. DeGroote is a pastor in the Baltimore-Washington United Methodist Conference.*

A member of my church recently dropped by my office. In the course of our conversation he mentioned that he was a member of the Ku Klux Klan. "We are just simply Christian people defending the Christian way of life," he said. And he meant it.

My response was brief and direct. "You can't be both Christian and a member of the KKK, or any other white supremacy group," I said. "They are contradictory patterns of living. When guided by one, we squeeze out the other." I now receive telephone calls from this person, designed to give me an opportunity to "reconsider" my position.

The KKK is but one of a collection of hate groups that coalesced into a coherent white supremacy movement in the 1990s. They were largely facilitated by the ease and low cost of Internet communications. The movement has interpreted changing economic and political conditions through a reformulation of old fears, hatreds, and conspiracy theories. Like a virus once thought under control, ideas and hatreds that racked the 20th century have mutated, ready to infect a new century. White supremacists build bridges to the ideas and activities of other groups, including Christians and our churches. The result is a growing white supremacist influence that is often difficult to detect.

Twisting Theology and Logic

Neo-Nazis and the Christian Identity churches are the two pillars of current white supremacy ideology. Neo-Nazis expand Hitler's myth of a biologically pure group called Aryans to claim that white Europeans represent an evolutionary superior class of beings, Jews excepted. They purport to use science for proof, but the scientific community rejects their claims. They attract followers

Peter L. DeGroote, "White Supremacists Cloak Bigotry in Theology," *Christian Social Action*, vol. 14, March/April 2001, pp. 14–16. Copyright © 2001 by *Christian Social Action*. Reproduced by permission.

by telling white people they are superior to and of greater worth than others. When the true findings of biology, in particular genetics, are ignored in our religious training and rejected by our traditions, the church lacks the tools to counter that attraction.

Christian Identity emerged out of Protestant Fundamentalism by two flights of biblical imagination. The first idea is that Jews are the descendants of Cain, who they assert was the product of an illicit relationship between the devil and Eve. Since Cain killed Abel, whites must be the descendants of the later children of Adam and Eve, children said to have been white and the original "chosen people" of the Bible. Exploiting an ancient legend, these white "chosen people" are said to be the lost tribes of Israel and that they migrated to Europe. Therefore, white Europeans are the real descendants of the "chosen people" of God. The apex of their migrations is now the United States. As a result, God has no further interest in Israel or Jerusalem. God's sole interest is in maintaining the United States as a white nation, a nation of God's "chosen."

A List of Enemies

Christian Identity's second flight of biblical imagination is that all whose ancestry is not white European are the descendants of animals. Calling Adam and Eve's creation the "Adamic" creation, all people of color are therefore products of the "pre-Adamic" creation. Putting the two fantasies together, everyone who is not of white European ancestry is diminished, either by classifying them as animals or, in the case of Jews, as representatives of evil.

With their fundamentalist roots, evolution is out of bounds with Christian Identity, so they applied their fantasy to biblical interpretation. They were helped along by the concepts of biblical inerrancy and the practice of using obscure texts to counter the general thrust of the biblical message. Arriving from different directions, neo-Nazis and Christian Identity came to the same conclusions about their enemies, the threats they face, and an agenda for the future.

The core list of enemies for all white supremacy groups include people of color, Jews, gay people, and feminists. (Our context requires noting that many Christian leaders express public antagonism toward the latter three.) A secondary list of enemies includes those who work for government, the media, international organizations, the United Nations, and similar groups. They are said to be part of a Jewish-created conspiracy called the

> *"Like a virus once thought under control, ideas and hatreds that racked the 20th century have mutated, ready to infect a new century."*

"new world order" that is dedicated to the destruction of the white race. This belief provided the rationale for the [1995] bombing of the federal office building in Oklahoma City. Even the children in the day care center were unimportant because they were the children of people who were, by virtue of their employment, traitors to their race.

Violence and Holy Wars

Public denial notwithstanding, white supremacy groups create an environment that encourages violence. Violence is often carried out in the name of a "Racial Holy War" (RAHOWA). Most of it is justified by the fantasy of self-defense in the conspiracy of an "undeclared racial war against the white race that is being carried out by the government and not reported by the Jewish controlled media."

The neo-Nazi rationale for violence is based on an ideology of political revolution. Christian Identity understands the so-called "undeclared racial war" as the beginnings of the war of tribulation so often associated with the return of Jesus. They differ with most fundamentalists, however, by believing that Jesus will come only at the end of the war, rather than at the beginning, to lead the final apocalyptic battle. Consequently, as the war has already begun, the coming of Jesus and his white kingdom depends on their going to war out of fear that the "new world order" might win before Jesus arrives.

The faithful must prepare the way for the coming Messiah. These religious motives are a particularly powerful stimulus for violence, as confirmed by similar versions of holy wars that are occurring around the world. For Christians who do not reflect on the end of time and the return of Jesus, this kind of thinking seems strange. Many do expect Jesus' return, however, and are not concerned about the details of the various hypotheses. Consequently, the Christian Identity version easily becomes mixed in with other versions—another bridge between white supremacy and Christianity.

> *"The core list of enemies for all white supremacy groups include people of color, Jews, gay people, and feminists."*

Neo-Nazis are opposed to democracy by definition. They argue that democracy might have had some value for whites during the early years of our nation, however, this began to wane when non-whites gained citizenship and, along with women, the right to vote. Coupling these developments with guarantees for equal protection under the law and the fruits of the civil rights movement, neo-Nazis conclude that it is necessary to overthrow the United States government before any further damage can be done. They are also convinced that it can be accomplished in this century, some believing it possible within 25 years.

Political Tactics

Typically, Christian Identity reaches the same conclusion about the need to overthrow the U.S. government, but by a different route. They proclaim that the original Constitution, with only its first 10 amendments, is the law of God for white people, God's "chosen," in the United States. Later amendments are a corruption of God's intentions, they say. Christian Patriots have worked out a body of doctrine they call "common law" built on the assertion that the later amendments to the Constitution, the enactment of federal statutes without approval of the states, and court decisions contrary to their view of the Constitution and the Bible have resulted in an illegitimate government. Emerging out of this view of defending the Constitution is a group of

> *"The religious and political views arising out of Christian Identity and their Patriot enforcers are similar to those used to support slavery."*

white supremacists called Christian Patriots. Called "militias" in the media because of their military style of organization, they understand themselves to be the defenders of God's law.

The religious and political views arising out of Christian Identity and their Patriot enforcers are similar to those used to support slavery and states rights before the Civil War and since. Christian Identity has provided hate groups with a source of renewed energy and has inspired the emergence of political movements publicly advancing the reestablishment of the Confederate States of America.

Two of the most recent to emerge are the League of the South and the Southern Party, both committed to the unique "traditions of religion of the South." The statement of purpose of the Southern Party, adopted in 1999, pledges to support state and local elected officials dedicated to the withdrawal of the 16 states of the original Confederacy from the United States and, when strong enough, to enact that objective.

Redefining Truth

Neo-Confederate groups have repackaged the old idea of white separatism. Calling it "white nationalism," they argue that they are not against anyone, they don't feel superior to or even hate anyone. Rather, they are only seeking to protect themselves and their families. Unable to explain what was unique about the "traditional society and religion of the South," other than chattel slavery, they simply conclude that whites and blacks (as well as others) should be separated. How they would go about doing this is not explained.

Another exercise in redefinition is worth noting. The word "racist" is often replaced by the word "racialism," which is supposed to be a positive concept to describe the common interests of white people. It helps whites to assert their superiority on the one hand, while providing the semantics to escape the racist label on the other.

Neo-Confederate websites and literature advance many theological and biblical ideas aimed at building bridges to Christians. For example, an article on the website for the National Organization for European Rights literally tears Paul's words in Galatians 3:26–29 (". . . there is no longer Jew nor Greek, slave nor free . . .") from their context. Most Christians find in that passage a biblical foundation for the principle that all humanity is one in Christ without regard to nation, race, culture, personal status, or gender. Countering that view, the website insists that Paul is writing about a "mystical/metaphysical" truth. It was never meant to take on social, political, or racial meaning in the present life, the website says. As it is a condition of eternity, one need not be concerned about such things "in this life." The connection between that notion and the promises once made to slaves, and others, that their lot in life would be rewarded in heaven is obvious.

A Return to the Past?

In the Church today there are many seeking to gain control of denominations and institutions by demanding a return to what they call the "central doctrines of classical Christianity." They bear the burden of demonstrating that they are not calling for a return to the same triumphal religious ideas that inaugurated Christian Europe to several centuries of oppression, subjugation, and enslavement of other peoples. The results of that were colonialism, cultural imperialism, genocide, slavery, segregation, and holocaust. They too thought of their violence as holy wars and their justifying language was not unlike the language of today's white supremacists.

Whatever might be meant by the "central doctrines of classical Christianity," it is well for Christians everywhere to pay heed to the central teachings of Jesus. One teaching concerns removing the log from our own eye before trying to take the sliver out of the eye of another. That visitor I had from the KKK was from my own church! Taking a stand against white supremacy may not help membership or attendance, but it will help to define what the Church of Jesus Christ stands for. Failure to take such a stand also sends a message in this time of resurgent white supremacy.

We need to acknowledge that the foundation of all of Jesus' teachings is to love God and others. Jesus' priority was to reach out to those denied the full benefits of society because they were judged unworthy of either honor or respect. We cannot claim love while maintaining our favorite little hates. Loving God has to include loving and respecting God. We are required as Christians to honor and respect others.

Racism Is Decreasing

by Deroy Murdock

About the author: *Deroy Murdock is a senior fellow with the Atlas Economic Research Foundation in Fairfax, Virginia.*

America's so-called "black leaders" seem to see a bigot under every bed. "Everywhere we see clear racial fault lines which divide American society as much now as at any time in our past," says [former] NAACP [National Association for the Advancement of Colored People] Chairman Julian Bond.

"Hardly an aspect of American life has escaped the baneful touch of this awful thing called racism," complains John Hope Franklin, chairman of President [Bill] Clinton's racial advisory board. "Wherever you go, you are going to see this." Ohio Democratic Rep. Louis Stokes simply declares: "Weary the victims of racism in this society."

But the greatest story never told is the tremendous progress Americans are making in race relations. From churches to the ballot box to the bedroom, Americans of various ethnicities are proving that—to paraphrase Rodney King—we all can just get along.

Jim Sleeper, author of *Liberal Racism*, believes there is a race industry that has a moral and financial stake in ginning up these racial bogeymen. As he says by phone: "There is a real effort to play up the bad news and play down the good. . . . The ground is shifting under our feet, and a lot of these people don't want to let go."

Alas, bigotry is not extinct. The James Byrd Jr. tragedy proved that. [On] June 7, [1998], three white ex-convicts picked up the disabled 49-year-old black man as he hitchhiked, chained him by the ankles to a pickup truck and dragged him to death.

This atrocity, however, overshadowed the racial harmony that once existed and soon reemerged in Jasper, Texas. Its black mayor, R.C. Horn, and black and white ministers alike, led 8,000 citizens in interracial rallies and joint prayer vigils. After one service, the mixed crowd hugged and sang "We Shall Overcome."

Deroy Murdock, "People in Mirror Are Less Racist than They Appear," *Insight*, vol. 14, November 23, 1998, p. 28. Copyright © 1998 by News World Communications, Inc. Reproduced by permission.

America Teaches Tolerance

The January 1997 murder of Ennis Cosby—son of comedian Bill Cosby and his wife, Camille—has been denounced as a bias crime. "I believe America taught our son's killer to hate African-Americans," Camille Cosby wrote in *USA Today*, adding, "Racism and prejudice are omnipresent and eternalized in America's institutions, media and myriad entities."

Ennis Cosby's senseless murder looks like a simple street crime perpetrated by Ukrainian immigrant Mikail Markhasev. While perhaps not an ethnic Eden, America mostly teaches tolerance to newcomers. Why did 40 percent of respondents recently select Bill Cosby as the nation's top dad if these truly are the United States of

> *"The greatest story never told is the tremendous progress Americans are making in race relations."*

Racism? Cosby's fans helped him earn $18 million [in 1997]. This demonstrated public fondness for Bill Cosby deflates his wife's theory of innate American bigotry.

For that matter, would white bigots vote for blacks? Whites increasingly choose blacks to represent them: New York State Comptroller Carl McCall; Ohio Treasurer Kenneth Blackwell; Colorado Secretary of State Vikki Buckley; Sen. Carol Moseley-Braun of Illinois; and former Virginia governor Douglas Wilder are examples of black Democrats and Republicans favored by heavily white electorates.

Despite these concrete achievements, some black politicians still see racially gerrymandered districts as the only way to secure electoral victories for blacks. In December 1995, the NAACP's Theodore Shaw predicted that, thanks to Supreme Court decisions against using race as the primary factor in reapportionment, "the Congressional Black Caucus will be able to meet in the back seat of a taxicab." Deval Patrick, then-assistant attorney general for civil rights, foresaw "a return to the days of all-white government." The Rev. Jesse Jackson feared a kind of ethnic cleansing.

Despite such overwrought rhetoric, all 35 black incumbent members of congress on the ballot in November 1996 were reelected, save one—Republican former Rep. Gary Franks of Connecticut, who lost to an opponent who called him an aloof slumlord. Franks' defeat was offset by Indianapolis Democrat Julia Carson, who won 53 percent of the vote in a 69 percent white district.

A Decrease in Anti-Semitism

While most racial discussions concern blacks and whites, dramatic decreases in anti-Semitism also highlight America's growing ethnic amity. The Anti-Defamatiom League, for example, documented 1,571 anti-Semitic crimes in 1997. That's an 8.8 percent drop from 1,722 such incidents in 1996.

Just two generations ago, Jewish entertainers routinely Anglicized their names. Alan Konigsberg morphed into Woody Allen, while Robert Zimmerman picked up his guitar and christened himself Bob Dylan.

Today, openly Jewish actors such as Jeff Goldblum and Julie Kavner fill movie screens. Few stars shine more brightly than Jerry Seinfeld. Without changing his surname to Sullivan or Stevens, Seinfeld headlined an obsessively beloved TV program, largely about New York City Jews. Indeed, its dialogue often lapsed into Yiddish, while its plots revolved around Jewish delicacies such as marble rye and chocolate babka.

NBC's hit, *Mad About You*, concerns a gentile (Helen Hunt) wed to a Jew (Paul Reiser). In this case, art imitates life: According to the 1990 National Jewish Population Survey, 52 percent of American Jews intermarry with gentiles.

One Jewish businessman in New York proudly tells me about his 4-year-old great nephew. The boy's mother is half-Jewish and half-Irish. His father's parents were born in Cuba. Despite having only one Jewish grandparent, he is active in his synagogue's youth club. "People will embrace Jewish culture, values and ethics even with mixed parents," the executive believes.

Interracial Marriage

Intermarriage thrives elsewhere. Among black men in 1970, for instance, 1.9 percent married white women. That figure more than quadrupled to 8.9 percent in 1993. In 1990, 28 percent of all marriages involving someone of Mexican ancestry also included a non-Hispanic. Half of Americans of Japanese descent marry people without Japanese roots. As John J. Miller predicts in his book, *The Unmaking of Americans*, "In the future, everyone will have a Korean grandmother."

"While perhaps not an ethnic Eden, America mostly teaches tolerance to newcomers."

[In June 1998], I led a small group of conferees from the Institute for Humane Studies at George Mason University to Atlanta, [Georgia's] Martin Luther King Jr. Center. These white college students and I, a 34-year-old black man, were equally stunned by the surreal Jim-Crow laws discussed at the Center. Louisiana, for instance, once required separate buildings for black and white residents at an institution for the blind.

That world might as well be Mars. Americans may never be as colorblind as those in that segregated home for the sightless. But across America, one thing grows clearer: The land where individuals "would not be judged by the color of their skin but by the content of their character"—as Dr. King put it—seems every day more a reality than a 35-year-old dream.

Racism Will Soon Disappear in America

by Orlando Patterson

About the author: *Orlando Patterson is a sociology professor at Harvard University and the author of* Rituals of Blood: Consequences of Slavery in Two American Centuries.

One can quibble with W.E.B. Du Bois's famous prediction for the twentieth century. [It was] not simply the century of the color line but a century of Jim Crow and myriad other persecutions—many within color boundaries. But, if Du Bois's epigraph was only half right, his modern-day disciples, who insist the color line will define the next 100 years as well, are altogether wrong. The racial divide that has plagued America since its founding is fading fast—made obsolete by migratory, sociological, and biotechnological developments that are already under way. By the middle of the twenty-first century, America will have problems aplenty. But no racial problem whatsoever.

Influential Social Patterns

For this we can thank four social patterns, each indigenous to a particular region of the country but which together will reshape the nation as a whole. The strongest and clearest might be called the California system. Cultural and somatic mixture will be its hallmark. A hybrid population, mainly Eurasian—but with a growing Latin element—will come to dominate the middle and upper classes and will grow exponentially, especially after the 2020s. Lower-class Caucasians, middle-class racial purists, and most African Americans, under pressure from an endless stream of unskilled Mexican workers, will move away. Those African Americans who remain will be rapidly absorbed into the emerging mixed population. The California system will come to dominate the American and Canadian Pacific Rim.

The second major pattern might be called the Caribbean-American system. Increasingly, the countries of the Caribbean basin will be socially and economi-

Orlando Patterson, "TRB from Washington: Race Over," *The New Republic*, January 10, 2000, p. 6.

cally integrated with the United States. As their fragile and already declining economies collapse (most dramatically in post-Castro Cuba), they will swarm the mainland by legal and illegal means. Florida will be the metropolitan center of this system, although Caribbean colonies will sprout all over the Northeast. Caribbean peoples will bring their distinctive concept of race and color to America, one in which people marry lighter and "white" as they move up the social ladder. This system will differ from the California one in that the dominant element will be Afro-Latin rather than Eurasian. Since the Caribbean is much closer than Asia, this system will also create a distinctive social type: genuinely transnational and post-national communities in which people feel equally at home in their native and American locations. Increasingly, people will spend their childhoods and retirements in the Caribbean and their productive years in America. The Caribbean-American system will compete with the African American community not only in the lower reaches of the labor force but as the nation's major source of popular culture, especially in music and sports. But, despite these differences, the Caribbean-American system, like the California one, will render the "one drop"[1] rule obsolete.

> *"The racial divide that has plagued America since its founding is fading fast."*

The third and most problematic system will be the one now emerging in the Northeast and urban Midwest. Here, the economic situation for all classes of African Americans and native-born Latinos is likely to deteriorate—with the ending of affirmative action, a shrinking public sector, and competition from skilled and unskilled (mainly Caribbean basin) immigrant labor. The rise of workfare without compensating provision for child care, combined with the growing pattern of paternal abandonment of children, will further undermine traditional family norms among African American, Latino, and, increasingly, the European American lower classes. Reversing the pattern that emerged after World Wax II, African Americans, Latinos, and the poorest Caucasians will move into the inner and secondary rings of what are now mainly European American middle-class suburbs. The middle classes will move to either gated exurbs or gentrified central cities—leaving a European American underclass that resembles other ethnic underclasses more and more.

Common Ground Based on Class

But, although these developments will at first exacerbate racial conflict, they will ultimately transform racial frustrations into class ones. Indeed, for the first time in the nation's history, young, poor, and alienated Caucasians, African Americans, and Latinos will find common ground—based on social resentment

1. A reference to the theory—common during the era of slavery and racial segregation in America—that having "one drop" of African blood defines an individual as black.

and a common lumpen-proletarian, hip-hop culture. Even as these young people periodically engage in murderous racial gang fights, intermarriage and miscegenation will escalate as the young poor of all races break away from present gender and racial taboos. In contrast to the California and Florida systems, the growing hybrid population in the Northeast and industrial Midwest will be lower-class, alienated, and out of control. But it will be hybrid nonetheless.

The exception will be in the Southeast, in what may be called the Atlanta pattern. African Americans and European Americans will cling to notions of racial purity and will remain highly (and voluntarily) segregated from each other. Affirmative action will be the bulwark of this system, the price the European American elite willingly pays for "racial" stability and the reassuring presence of a culturally familiar but socially distant African American group and a pliant working class. The old Confederacy will remain a place where everyone knows who is white and who is black and need reckon with no in-between. But, as opposed to the nineteenth and twentieth centuries, when the South defined the terms of racial engagement on which the entire nation interacted (more or less brutally), in the twenty-first century the Southern model will become an increasingly odd and decreasingly relevant anachronism.

For the decline of race as a factor in American life will result not only from immigration, which can perhaps be halted, but also from biotechnology. More and more in the coming decades, Americans will gain the means to genetically manipulate human appearance. The foundations of genetic engineering are already in place. Given the interest of the affluent population in male-pattern baldness, the restoration of hair loss after cancer treatment, and cancer-free tanning, science is likely to create dramatic new methods of changing hair texture and skin color. Indeed, in November 1999, scientists at Columbia University transplanted scalp cells from one person to another. I don't expect many African Americans to chose straight-haired whiteness for themselves or their progeny, but many will opt for varying degrees of hybridity. In a world dominated by mass culture, many will embrace changes that enhance their individuality. Once dramatically manipulable by human action, "race" will lose its social significance, and the myth of racial purity will be laid to rest.

> *"Intermarriage and miscegenation will escalate as the young poor of all races break away from present gender and racial taboos."*

By the middle of the twenty-first century, the social virus of race will have gone the way of smallpox. The twenty-first century, relieved of the obscuring blinkers of race, will be a century of class and class consciousness, forcing the nation to finally take seriously its creed that all are created equal. It should be interesting.

Conservatives Are Wrongly Accused of Racism

by Samuel Francis

About the author: *Samuel Francis is a nationally syndicated columnist.*

The tedium that descended upon the nation's politics last winter [of 2000] when [George] Bush II ascended the presidential throne was relieved briefly in the waning days of the Clinton era by the bitter breezes that wafted around some of the new President's Cabinet appointments. After repeatedly muttering his meaningless campaign slogan, "I'm a uniter, not a divider," Mr. Bush suddenly found himself accused of the horrid and unpardonable offense of dividing when he nominated certain individuals of whom the real rulers of the country did not approve. "Uniting," as the former governor of Texas should have known and probably did know, means doing what the *Zeitgeist*[1] (and those who craft it) want; "dividing" means doing what they don't want, and some of the cabinet nominees seemed for a short time to be the kind of undesirables who entertain ideas of their own and harbor sneaky inclinations to act on them. For a few weeks, it was uncertain whether the President would cave in to the demand of his political opponents in Congress and the mass media and dump the objectionable nominees or whether he and the nominees would contrive some means of placating their foes and persuading them they had no intention of bucking their wishes or challenging their power. What was never even contemplated, of course, was that the President and his prospective ministers would defy their critics and actually dare assert their own authority and leadership.

The most controversial of the Cabinet nominees was former Missouri Senator John Ashcroft, whose opposition to a Clinton-appointed black judge as well as several other thoughtcrimes immediately sparked the predictable accusations of "racism," "white supremacy," and "insensitivity." A black former congressman,

---

1. spirit of the time

Missouri Democrat William Clay, mocked Mr. Bush's professions of "reaching out" to blacks by comparing Mr. Ashcroft's appointment to the Ku Klux Klan's attempts to reach out "to blacks with nooses and burning crosses," while a small-time left-wing witch hunter in Missouri breathlessly declared that "an examination of Ashcroft's recent record shows that he has actively cultivated ties to white supremacists and extreme hate groups." The "white supremacists and extreme hate groups" turned out to be merely the *Southern Partisan*, a Confederate heritage periodical whose editor-in-chief last year [in 2000] ran the South Carolina presidential campaign of Sen. John McCain. (It's interesting that Honest John never once opened his trap to defend either his ally or his

> *"'Racism' is simply a set of beliefs or actions that oppose a certain political agenda, and that agenda is largely initiated by . . . non-whites."*

ally's magazine.) This "linkage" was soon turned into political fodder on which the media, the Congressional Black Caucus, and Senate Democrats were able to browse for several weeks.

Mr. Ashcroft was confirmed as attorney general, but only because he danced to the tunes called by his and the new President's enemies. The nominee hastened to repudiate any sympathies for the Confederacy, its leadership, or its political heritage that his interview with the *Partisan* might have suggested. "Slavery is abhorrent," Mr. Ashcroft gushed to his inquisitors. "Abraham Lincoln is my favorite president . . . I would have fought with General Ulysses Grant . . . I believe that racism is wrong."

Of course, at no time in his life had Mr. Ashcroft, who seems to be a dim but decent enough chap, ever uttered any thought or opinion that would insinuate he believed "racism" in any conventional or traditional meaning to be right. However vague the word has always been, its traditional usage generally had something to do with race and the claim by members of one race that another race was in some sense inferior—intellectually, morally, etc. By the conventional meaning, not only is Mr. Ashcroft not guilty, but his critics were not able to produce any evidence whatsoever to suggest that he was. At the most, they merely inferred his supposed beliefs about race from his stated views about the Confederacy and his various "links" with people and groups who also were never shown to be "racist."

The New Meaning of "Racism"

A few weeks after the Ashcroft hearings, yet another controversy about "racism" erupted, this time on American college campuses. Neoconservative activist David Horowitz placed a series of ads in college newspapers arguing against the budding movement in support of reparations for slavery. Mr. Horowitz's ads, probably deliberately designed to be innocuous, offered ten reasons why reparations are "a bad idea *for blacks*—and racist" to boot. Some college newspapers actually dared to publish the ads and, not infrequently, soon found themselves under siege for their own "racism." At the University of Wisconsin's *Badger Herald*, a mob demanded the resignation of the editor, sporting signs with the slogan, "*Badger Herald* Racist."

Similar incidents are well known, both on college campuses and elsewhere, but the point is that what the targets are being accused of has nothing whatsoever to do with what they have said or thought or done about race as a biological or social phenomenon. "Racism" today has nothing to do with race; it has to do with politics. "Racism" is simply a set of beliefs or actions that oppose a certain political agenda, and that agenda is largely initiated by and closely associated with nonwhites and pushed by their white allies.

Thus, opposing reparations, as the mob indicated, is itself a "racist" act—not because the opponents of reparations think all blacks are naturally inferior and therefore should have been and should still be slaves, but simply because reparations are now part of the black racial-political agenda, and anyone who opposes that agenda is a racist. Opposing affirmative action is also racist—not because its opponents are said to hate blacks and other nonwhites and want to repress and exploit them, but for *any* reason. The same is largely true of supporting Confederate flags and symbols or opposing immigration or arguing in favor of "racial profiling" by police. Back in the 1980's, white South Africans would tell me that "apartheid" had been largely abolished in their country and that even radical critics, black or white, would have to recognize that truth. I always tried to make them see that "abolishing apartheid" had nothing to do with racial equality, that their critics had little interest in that, and that what they really wanted was black domination. "Apartheid" would cease to exist not when South African blacks were able to eat in desegregated restaurants and vote in parliamentary elections but only when they had taken over the government of the country—which is exactly what happened. "Apartheid" ended the day Nelson Mandela and his Communist Party–dominated African National Congress came to power, and not a moment before.

> *"You can argue against affirmative action because it's inherently unjust to everyone . . . but it doesn't matter. You are still a 'racist' and a supporter of 'white supremacy.'"*

A Political Redefinition

"Racism," concisely redefined, is merely opposition to nonwhite power or to any measure that promises such power or support for any measure or institution that thwarts such power. The rationale behind the new meaning of the word is the claim that in American, Western, or white societies, nonwhites are—by definition—subordinate groups, and the dominant society is therefore (also by definition) "white supremacist." It is not necessarily white supremacist because of the formal legal and political structure (as in South Africa under apartheid or the segregated South), any more than it is "racist" because of the particular ideological rationalization of the domination. "Racism" in this sense is no longer confined to those who adhere to hereditarian views of intelligence and behavior. That is one form of the new racism, but by no means the only one. In the ideological *Weltanschauung* [worldview] from which the new meaning is derived, scientific theories and empirical studies that depict nonwhites as being in some respects inferior to whites are merely one means by which white dominance is rationalized, but religious, moral, social, historical, and other nonscientific rationales are also available and tend to be favored by the white ruling class over the rationale of biological "racism." The liberal-neoconservative ideal of a "color-blind society" is also racist, because it is used to reject measures like affirmative action that empower nonwhites. By the same reasoning, nonwhites themselves can also be "racists"—[Supreme Court Justice] Clarence Thomas springs to mind—as the white ruling class conscripts and rewards nonwhites willing to offer justifications for their domination. Moreover, opposition to "hate crime" legislation, "sensitivity" training, immigration, any "civil rights" measure, law, or policy, or to anything else the nonwhite agenda demands is also racist, regardless of the reasons offered. You can argue against affirmative action because it's inherently unjust to everyone or support the Confederate flag because not many white Confederates owned slaves or be against reparations because they are bad for blacks or oppose immigration because it increases population growth or for whatever other reasons you can concoct, but it doesn't matter. You are still a "racist" and a supporter of "white supremacy" because what you want to do or stop doing thwarts nonwhite power.

The new meaning of "racism" is not a verbal trick or a political charade. It derives logically from the worldview that regards the dominant society as repressive and exploitative of nonwhites for the benefit of whites, and, granted its premises, it makes at least as much sense as the older and more conventional meaning of the word. Indeed, the new meaning becomes increasingly obvious as we see how the term is actually used and deployed against political figures like Mr. Ashcroft, President Bush, or Justice Thomas.

Conservatives and "Racism"

Still, the new meaning is not as obvious as it should be, for the simple reason that "conservatives"—I use the term in its broadest possible meaning, to include Mr. Bush and Mr. Ashcroft and Mr. Horowitz—still don't get it. They don't get it because their tactics in fighting the racially tinged measures they oppose seem always to presuppose the old definition of the word and therefore to aim at all costs at not being tarred with the "racist" label. Let's get a black nominee or spokesman; then they can't possibly accuse us of being racists. Let's not use hereditarian arguments but just talk about the "culture"; then they can't possibly accuse us of being racists. Let's not say reparations or affirmative action or immigration or sanctions on South Africa are bad for whites or for white Western societies and civilization, but say instead they're bad for blacks, for immigrants, for nonwhites; then they can't possibly accuse us of being racists.

The problem, of course, is that they do always accuse you of being racists, despite your pathological phobia of being so called and the bizarre lengths to which you are willing to go, distorting and weakening your own case, to avoid and deny the accusation. They accuse you of being racists precisely because, no matter what you say or how you say it, you are, by the new meaning of the term, exactly that. You may oppose the nonwhite political agenda for precisely the reasons you offer—because it really is, by your values, bad for blacks or immigrants or the environment or simply unjust—but the reasons don't matter, and no one on the other side of the racial power struggle gives a hoot about them. What they do give a hoot about is the triumph of their agenda and the power it will yield, and anyone who is not on board with that agenda, for whatever reasons they offer, is a "racist" and an apologist for "white supremacy."

> *"Much of the purpose of the new meaning [of racism] is precisely to demonize and delegitimize conservatism of any kind."*

Failure to recognize the new meaning of "racism" therefore constitutes a serious vulnerability on the part of those who oppose the nonwhite agenda, because by planning their strategy as though the conventional meaning of "racism" still applied, they do nothing to avoid the charge of "racism" in its new meaning and waste an immense amount of their time and energies trying to avoid being identified as "racists" in any sense. Their enemies can then avoid any serious debate about the issues on their agenda and spend all their time lobbing accusations and making the opponents of the agenda jump through hoops—which is exactly what Mr. Ashcroft did and what Mr. Bush has been doing ever since he was elected. But the new, political meaning of "racism" is so broad that it effectively strips the word of the old pejorative associations that serious political figures understandably wish to avoid. Under the new meaning, the term has no more pejorative connotation than "conservative" or "liberal"; indeed, it is more or less identical with the former term, and much of the purpose of the new meaning is precisely to demonize and delegitimize conservatism of any kind. Nevertheless, the word only retains any negative implications because of its linkages to the old meaning—which is why it survives at all in the national political lexicon—not because of the actual content of the new one.

Conservatives who seriously oppose the nonwhite political agenda (as serious conservatives will and should) can therefore expect to be called "racists," and while it is not useful to court the label, the new meaning it has acquired removes any compelling reason to avoid it, and certainly any reason to obsess over it. As the revolutionary and totalitarian character of the antiwhite racial-political agenda becomes more and more obvious, those who push that agenda will discover that the "racists" who oppose them are more and more numerous, until what they falsely call "racism"—so far from being "extremist" or a "fringe" movement—has evolved into the political and cultural mainstream, and conservatives of every stripe will say, "We are all 'racists' now."

Chapter 2

Is Racism Institutionalized in Society and Culture?

Chapter Preface

People often define racism as an individual's belief that one race is superior to another or as a person's overt hatred of another because of racial and cultural differences. However, many contemporary analysts believe that the most profound and widespread forms of racism are institutional rather than interpersonal. The phrase "institutionalized racism" is sometimes used to describe the policies of an organization that is deliberately racist—such as the Gestapo in Nazi Germany or South Africa's police during that nation's years of apartheid. More often, though, institutional racism is used to describe a form of discrimination that is systemic and often hidden or inadvertent. James Jones, author of *Prejudice and Racism*, defines institutional racism as "those established laws, customs and practices which systematically reflect and produce racial inequalities." Such racism occurs when rules, regulations, and manners are discriminatory in effect, though not necessarily in intention.

Most civil rights advocates maintain that the best way to detect institutional racism is to collect statistical data that is delineated by race, ethnicity, and immigrant status. In May 2000, a coalition of civil rights groups filed a class action lawsuit against the state of California in response to the apparent inequities in the state's school system. "The plaintiff's complaint describes more than 100 schools," explain educators Terry Keleher and Tammy Johnson, "where at least half the teaching staff is not fully credentialed. Many schools have outdated textbooks and lack ample classroom seating, while others lack bathrooms and ventilation." The proof of institutional racism lies in the fact that these poorly equipped schools serve "mostly students of color in urban areas, exemplifying the fact that students of different races frequently experience very separate and unequal educational opportunities." Students attending these schools are less likely to excel academically, which in turn affects their future college and career potential. In addition, these educational disparities reinforce the stereotype that blacks and Latinos are underachieving or intellectually inferior, analysts point out.

Yet some commentators disagree with the concept of "disparate impact," what the Supreme Court defines as the observation of unintentionally discriminatory outcomes, as a way to detect racism. Underachieving students could be affected by other factors—family economic status, extracurricular activities, or parental involvement—independent of race, these analysts maintain. According to Roger Clegg, vice president of the Washington, D.C.–based Center for Equal Opportunity, real institutional discrimination is rare, but because the Supreme Court allows lawsuits based on disparate impact, "mere circumstantial evidence of discrimination is sufficient to win a case." In Clegg's opinion the disparate impact approach to racism encourages "the already widespread tendency . . . to view every social problem through a racial lens. If a disproportion exists, then it must be caused by race, says the Right, or racism, says the Left. But racism is not the problem, on the one hand, nor is there 'something in the blood' that predisposes some groups toward antisocial behavior or underachievement." In the end, Clegg argues, such a "minority-versus-white" worldview allows racial resentment and stereotypes to flourish.

The fact that both the U.S. Supreme Court and Congress support the disparate-impact approach to civil rights law suggests that the concept of institutional racism is taken seriously by America's government and legal institutions. However, as some of the viewpoints in the following chapter reveal, these institutions themselves are often accused of systemic racism. Whether or not this form of racism is prevalent will likely be debated in the years to come as competing interests shape and reshape civil rights law.

Racism Is Endemic in the Juvenile Justice System

by Hugh B. Price

About the author: *Hugh B. Price is president of the National Urban League, a community service agency that aims to eliminate institutional racism in the United States.*

Civil rights leaders like Jesse Jackson, political officeholders, and many others throughout black America have said for years that Jim Crow is alive and well in America's criminal justice system.

They've criticized the harsher sentences imposed on African-Americans arrested for possession of crack cocaine, compared with those imposed on whites arrested for possession of powdered cocaine. They've questioned the disproportionate number of African-Americans on the death rows of the nation's prisons.

Now, a new study sponsored by the Department of Justice and six national foundations adds startling new information to the growing evidence that racism is endemic in the juvenile justice system as well.

The report, "And Justice for Some," shows that African- and Hispanic-American youth are treated more severely than white teens charged with comparable crimes at every step of the juvenile justice system.

The former are more likely than their white counterparts to be arrested, held in jail, sent to juvenile or adult court, convicted and given longer prison terms.

Blatant Bias

Indeed, the report presents evidence of bias so blatant that it's mind-boggling. For example:

• Among teens who've not been sent to prison before, blacks are more than six times as likely as whites to be sentenced by juvenile court judges to prison.

• For those young people charged with a violent crime who've never been in juvenile prison, black teens are nine times more likely than whites to be sentenced to juvenile prison.

• For those charged with drug offenses, black youths are 48 times more likely than whites to be sentenced to juvenile prison.

• White youth charged with violent offenses are incarcerated on average for 193 days after trial. By contrast, black youth are incarcerated an average of 254 days; Hispanic youth, an average of 305 days.

• Nationally blacks under the age of 18 make up 15 percent of their age group, but 26 percent of those young people arrested, 31 percent of those sent to juvenile court, 44 percent of those detained in juvenile jails and 32 percent of those found guilty of being a delinquent.

> *"Jim Crow is alive and well in America's criminal justice system."*

• Young blacks account for 46 percent of all juveniles tried in adult criminal courts, 40 percent of those sent to juvenile prisons and 58 percent of all juveniles confined in adult prisons.

Juvenile Injustice

These and other alarming statistics underscore that the nation is faced with an extraordinarily serious social and civil rights issue: We have a juvenile justice system that dispenses juvenile injustice.

"When you look at this data, it is undeniable that race is a factor," said Mark Soler, president of the Youth Law Center, a research and advocacy group in Washington. The center led the coalition of civil rights and youth advocacy organizations (including the National Urban League), which organized the research project.

Soler added that the biased, harsher treatment of teens of color who get in trouble with the law has a continuing, devastating impact on their prospects for a decent life, making it harder and harder for those ensnared in its web to "go straight"—to "complete their education, get jobs and be good husbands and fathers."

In addition to the Justice Department, support for the research effort came from the Ford Foundation, the MacArthur Foundation, the Rockefeller Foundation, the Walter Johnson Foundation, the Annie E. Casey Foundation, and the Center on Crime, Communities and Culture of George Soro's Open Society Institute.

The national study closely tracks the findings of another study, "The Color of Justice," released in February [2000] by the non-profit Justice Policy Institute that examined the juvenile justice system in California.

Dan Macallair, the institute's co-director and the study's co-author, told *The New York Times*, "California has a double standard: throw kids of color behind bars, but rehabilitate white kids who commit comparable crimes."

This double standard at both the state and national level has continued, and perhaps grown even sharper as juvenile crime has declined in recent years as precipitously as adult crime.

Obviously, all Americans can be grateful for such declines, and for the efforts law enforcement agencies and community and other organizations have made to establish and maintain the peace and help teens be law-abiding. And, we're not naive. We realize that many young people who run afoul of the law probably have committed some offense. Some of them would never be mistaken for angels.

But none of that explains or excuses these blatant disparities in the way the criminal justice system handles, on the one hand, black, Hispanic and Asian-American youngsters, and, on the other, white youngsters who commit the same offenses.

[Former] Attorney General Janet Reno deserves kudos for helping to expose the rampant racism in juvenile sentencing. The question we all have to answer now is how we act quickly to get the "juvenile injustice system" to clean up its act.

Environmental Racism Threatens Minorities

by Robert Bullard, interviewed by Jim Motavalli

About the authors: *Robert Bullard teaches sociology and chairs the Environmental Justice Resource Center at Clark Atlanta University. Jim Motavalli is the editor of* E: The Environmental Magazine, *a bimonthly journal.*

When, in 1979, Dr. Robert Bullard wrote a study called *Solid Waste Sites and the Black Houston Community*, nobody had heard of environmental racism. . . . It would be three more years before anyone used that phrase, but Dr. Bullard had plainly made the connection between toxic siting and communities of color, leading to the first lawsuit, *Bean v. Southwestern Waste Management*, (filed by his wife) that used civil rights law to challenge environmental discrimination. By 1991, when Bullard helped plan the first National People of Color Environmental Leadership Summit in Washington, D.C., the fight for environmental justice was well-established, with activists from around the country making common cause with each other.

Dr. Bullard is the author or editor of three landmark texts, *Confronting Environmental Racism* (1993), *Dumping on Dixie* (1994) and *Unequal Protection* (1996). He serves on the Environmental Protection Agency's National Advisory Council for Environmental Policy and Technology, offering direction on complaints filed under the anti-discriminatory Title VI of the Civil Rights Act of 1964.

Dr. Bullard, who teaches sociology and heads the Environmental Justice Resource Center at Clark Atlanta University, has become the country's leading authority on toxic discrimination. His most recent book is *Just Transportation*, a look at barriers to mobility in minority communities. Dr. Bullard says he's heartened by recent decisions showing the federal government taking an increasingly activist role against do-nothing state environmental agencies that collaborate with polluters. Environmental racism isn't going away, he says, but communities are banding together to fight it and, in many cases, winning.

The Concept of Environmental Racism

Jim Motavalli: Maybe we can start with the general concept of environmental racism, where the term originated and how it has come into broad acceptance.

Robert Bullard: The phrase "environmental racism" was coined back in 1982 by Reverend Ben Chavis, then the director of the United Church of Christ's Commission for Racial Justice (CRJ). He was talking about Warren County, North Carolina, and the siting of a toxic waste landfill in that predominantly black county. People saw that the only reason Warren County was selected was because it was poor and black. The process by which that happens has now been codified and defined in all kinds of reports and books. Basically, environmental racism is another form of institutionalized discrimination.

In 1987, CRJ published a report entitled *Toxic Wastes and Race in the United States*, which looked at the siting of hazardous waste sites by race and income. It concluded that the most important factor in locating these facilities was race.

Before that time, was there very little awareness of this as an issue?

There was a lot of awareness in terms of local communities. As a matter of fact, in 1979 my wife filed a lawsuit in Houston, Texas, charging the city and one of the largest national waste companies, Browning Ferris Industries, with environmental discrimination in siting its facilities. And that was the first environmental justice lawsuit filed under the Civil Rights Act of 1964. But most of the awareness was

> *"Environmental racism is another form of institutionalized discrimination."*

local. There was no pulling together of the fact that African-American children are poisoned with lead in their homes and on the playgrounds at a greater rate than any other group. And this is one of the reasons why kids are dropping out of school, put in classes for the retarded, and told they're slow learners.

Where the freeways go, where the landfills and the bus barns are, that's where you'll find environmental injustice. And it wasn't until people started to meet and talk and share their notes that we saw this national pattern. And we began to see that environmental racism is more than where the garbage dump is, it's all those other things, too.

Convent, Louisiana

In Convent, Louisiana, there is an incredible concentration of plants in a very small black community. There's just been a precedent-setting ruling in which the EPA [Environmental Protection Agency] is actually holding up state licensing of the proposed Shintech polyvinyl chloride (PVC) plastics plant there. Maybe you could talk about how significant that is and the implications if this plant is not licensed.

The fact is that this community is already over-burdened with polluting facilities. It has a dozen already, and 60 percent unemployment there, so there is certainly no correlation between the number of facilities and the jobs they allegedly create. The Title VI case is now being looked at by the EPA, and it's very important. This is our *Brown v. Board of Education*, as significant as that ruling desegregating public schools. If we can't win in Convent, we might as well throw in the towel. So there's a lot of eyes that will be looking at Convent, especially since President Bill Clinton's 1994 executive order reinforcing Title VI on his watch.

> *"Where the freeways go, where the landfills and the bus barns are, that's where you'll find environmental injustice."*

Title VI says no federal funds can be used to discriminate based on race or color, and that the law has to be used to enforce equal protection when it comes to housing, education, employment and voting. The president [Bill Clinton] was saying that now's the time for us to do a better job of enforcing our environmental laws equally across the board. The order also reinforces the National Environmental Policy Act, which was passed by Congress in 1969. The Act says that before any type of operation can go in that may have a negative impact on the environment or on health, a socioeconomic impact assessment must be done.

In Chester, Pennsylvania, the local citizens' group has also won an order allowing them to continue with their civil rights suit against the state.

The Chester case is very important because the city is inundated with all kinds of toxic waste facilities. That community basically said that it's had enough, and it filed suit. Chester is almost 75 percent black, and it has a large low-income population. They've won their case so far, getting a state judge to say that their complaint can be heard under Title VI.[1] There was another case similar to that in Flint, Michigan [in 1997]. The predominately black community there filed suit to stop an incinerator, saying that the state of Michigan didn't even require this company coming in to do an environmental impact assessment. So the community sued and won, with the state judge saying that the state of Michigan has an obligation to protect all of its citizens.

Polluters Provide Few Economic Benefits

That brings up something that seems to me to be a pattern in the communities I visited. Typically, the local residents not only don't have a voice in siting these plants, they're also in the dark about what the plants really do.

Exactly. Most of these communities have no idea what these facilities are, or the kinds of emissions and pollution that will be coming from them. Most of these facilities don't even hire people that live in the community. So the com-

1. This lawsuit was filed against the Pennyslvania Department of Environmental Protection after it granted a permit to build a soil treatment facility in Chester. The case was appealed to the U.S. Supreme Court in 1998, but was declared moot after the soild treatment company abandoned plans to build a plant in Chester.

munity really doesn't have anything to gain by having these facilities next door. People could walk to work at the 12 plants in Convent, but you have a 60 percent unemployment rate.

These companies also get tax breaks, which means they don't really provide much in the way of economic relief, either.

They don't provide much in terms of anything, except for the very few people who commute in, get the jobs and leave. This has never really been closely examined before, and that's why I say, look at Chester, Convent and Flint, because they're very significant. There's another case that should be studied, because it's an example of communities that aren't polluted yet. It's Forest Grove and Center Springs in northwest Louisiana. The communities got together, formed Citizens Against Nuclear Trash, and decided that they would not accept a proposed $700 million uranium enrichment plant that was going to be built in the middle of the road separating them. The facility would have been so large that people would have had to drive nine miles around to the other community. This is the arrogance the company, Louisiana Energy Services, had. These communities, which were founded in 1860 and 1910, were treated like they were invisible, and not even listed in the environmental impact statements.

In May of [1997], the judges from the Nuclear Regulatory Licensing Board denied the plant a permit based on environmental justice grounds. In April of [1998], the NRC [Nuclear Regulatory Committee] upheld the board's decision and denied that permit on appeal. Now I hear the company has packed up and left. The plant, which would have been the first privately owned uranium enrichment plant in the country, will not be built.

Are we going to see that uranium plant appear somewhere else now, in another impoverished community?

I doubt it. In the process of gathering the data, we established that this facility was not only dangerous and sited in a very racist way, it was not even needed. We don't need any more enriched uranium. It's already being produced by the Department of Energy, and no new nuclear power plants are being built.

States Collaborate with Industry

Another problem is that the state departments of environmental protection, particularly in Texas and Louisiana, appear to be very much collaborating with industry. They seem to see their roles as helping new industries get established. Is this a pattern you've seen?

Of course. There are very few of these departments that act as advocates for communities, that are aggressive in making sure that environmental justice exists. There's a lack of understanding that the state should be operating for the benefit of all its citizens, not just the most powerful ones. You'll find these agency heads going in and out of jobs with industry. That's why people look to the federal EPA to really hold these state agencies' feet to the fire. As the feds move more of their federal mandates down to the states for enforcement, we're going to see more of these challenges.

In New Mexico, I visited with former uranium miners in Shiprock. They say they've been unfairly compensated for the 50 years they were subjected to radiation, and are pressing Congress to enact a new benefits package.

Whether we talk about the miners in New Mexico, or the nuclear dump proposed for California's Ward Valley, which would also affect Native Americans, or the Sierra Blanca nuclear dump in Texas, in a mostly Hispanic area, there's clearly a pattern of attacks on communities of color, and they're forming alliances. The Navajos are not alone, and the people of Ward Valley are not alone. It's a signal that the environmental justice movement has matured, and we can tap into each other's resources, experiences and expertise. It's not enough, today, for a community to hire a lawyer and try to fight these very powerful institutions on its own. It needs a team approach. In Convent, a whole lot of organizations are working together on the national issues, including Greenpeace, the Tulane Environmental Law Clinic, and the Deep South Center for Environmental Justice, and that has allowed the community to organize and have an impact locally. We get accused of being outsiders, but the communities don't see it that way; they value the assistance.

> *"There's clearly a pattern of attacks on communities of color."*

What can you do for a community like Convent that has been so effectively poisoned already, with a dozen plants, that stopping Shintech's PVC facility won't change that much?

That's the point we've been making all along. Winning the Shintech case won't be the end of it. There's still an environmental justice issue in Convent, because of the concentration of polluters and the proposals that are pending. We have to talk now about targeted enforcement and compliance. We need the state Department of Environmental Quality, and the federal EPA, to closely examine what's happening in that community in terms of emissions, and study the cumulative effects. It is possible for companies to be in compliance, but the overall situation to be highly dangerous. We should see an aggressive waste minimization and emissions reduction program, and in some cases we may have to change production processes. The next battle is coming up with a standard that says that Convent's toxic burden has been reached.

Do you agree with the adage that "waste attracts waste"?

It is very common for an industrial polluting plant to go in, and after that only other plants like it come into the area. Once you get one, it's easy to get another, and when there's two, there soon is three. You don't get these types of incinerators and chemical plants being compatible with clean industries or office towers. To create white-collar office jobs you have to attract the population, and usually people like to live near where they work.

When the toxic landfill came into Warren County, North Carolina, giving birth to the environmental justice movement, the county started to lose major businesses, because people started to identify the county with hazardous wastes.

In Chester, municipal corruption is a major factor in the siting of these plants. How big a role do you think kickbacks and under-the-table arrangements play in what gets built?

When we look at the political process on the local or state level, we always find corrupt politicians willing to do the bidding of industry. Whoever industry can buy off or pay off, they'll do that, because it's about money. The politicians then take on the role of trying to sell these industries to the community—but, increasingly, it doesn't fly. The communities have right on their side, and in many instances they've been able to withstand all the cash and the temptations.

The Republican Party Panders to Racist Sentiments

by Nicholas Confessore

About the author: *Nicholas Confessore is the senior correspondent for the* American Prospect, *a biweekly liberal journal of opinion.*

It wasn't surprising that during the [2001] fight over [Republican] John Ashcroft's nomination for attorney general, one side seemed especially eager to discuss his putative racism while the other side eschewed the matter. But it was surprising that his defenders were the eager ones. "I have never known John Ashcroft to be a racist," proclaimed Oklahoma Representative J.C. Watts, who testified on Ashcroft's behalf. "It is not pleasant for me to hear terms such as racism applied to you," sniffed Bob Smith, sometime-Republican senator of New Hampshire, with a nod to his old colleague. "Branding a good man with the ugly slur of 'racist' without justification or cause is intolerable," Missouri Republican Kenny Hulshof told the Senate Judiciary Committee.[1]

But who, exactly, was branding Ashcroft a racist? "Let me be very clear about one thing," Democratic Senate Judiciary Committee chairman Patrick Leahy announced when he gaveled to order the first day of hearings. "This is not about whether Senator Ashcroft is racist, anti-Catholic, anti-Mormon, or anti-anything else. Those of us who have worked with him in the Senate do not make that charge." He was echoed, over the following three days, by most of Ashcroft's chief critics, including Senators Charles Schumer ("You know, I don't believe Senator Ashcroft is a racist"), Joseph Biden ("I find you a man of honesty and integrity"), Dick Durbin ("I have not accused Senator Ashcroft of racial prejudice, nor will I"), and, for that matter, Ronnie White, the African-American jurist whom Ashcroft had once defamed as being "pro-criminal" ("I

---

1. John Ashcroft was appointed U.S. Attorney General in 2000.

don't think John Ashcroft is a racist"). Indeed, even the most vehement Democrats seemed muzzled as they tried to explain what, exactly, was so objectionable about this honest, experienced, nonracist man of integrity.

Political Racism

How have we arrived at such a pass? . . . The Republicans claimed to be
shocked, shocked, that Ashcroft "would have to endure comments about racism
and segregation," as Smith complained. But the party of [Abraham] Lincoln, as
Republicans are fond of calling themselves these days, has become the party of
[former pro-segregation senators] Strom Thurmond and Jesse Helms. And
therein lies the problem.

The Republican Party is not demonstrably racist; nor is conservatism. Nor are
Republican politicians generally; nor are Republican voters generally. But the
electoral history of the GOP over the past four decades has largely been one of
assimilation: first drawing large numbers of voters with deep racial animus
(along with many unreconstructed racists) from the Democratic Party in the
South, then absorbing that bloc into the GOP's political base, and, finally, finding tactful ways to keep them there while simultaneously appealing to other,
more tolerant voters. And it's that last part—trying to attract racially progressive moderates without losing the party's racially antagonistic constituency—
that has so confused the essential question hovering around the Ashcroft hearings: What does it take to be a racist in politics today?

There was a time when the Democratic Party tolerated people more objectionable than John Ashcroft among its own ranks. But most of them began to
leave during the 1960s and 1970s, disgusted with the party's embrace of the
civil rights movement. Seeing an opportunity, the Republican Party rolled out
the welcome mat via Richard Nixon's infamous Southern Strategy—that is, deliberate appeals to reactionary southern voters. (Once the South was placed on
the road to Republicanization, GOP strategists like Lee Atwater crafted a com-
plementary Northern Strategy, which involved provoking the simmering tension
between blacks and working-class white ethnics and dislodging the latter from
their traditional berth in the Democratic Party.) The Southern Strategy remained
standard practice for Republicans even into the 1980s. Back then, Republicans
offered far more than speeches to Bob Jones University, the now infamous institution that equates Catholicism with Satanism and only recently ended its
ban on interracial dating. In 1982 the [Republican] Reagan administration actually joined the university in a lawsuit aimed at granting tax-exempt status to
racially discriminatory—that is, racist—private schools and colleges.

A Racial Wedge Strategy

But by the mid-1980s, changing public mores accompanied a new political
generation that came to the fore; open alliance with explicitly racist groups, institutions, and causes became verboten. In its place, a certain political melange

began to emerge, a kind of code language: fervent support for "states' rights," veneration of Jefferson Davis and the antebellum culture, and vilification of Abraham Lincoln and Martin Luther King, Jr. (always as a philanderer, never as a civil rights leader per se). Usefully, the code was officially, explicitly non-racist. When Trent Lott gave an interview to the *Southern Partisan* in 1984 and was asked what he meant when he told the Sons of Confederate Veterans that "the spirit of [Confederate president] Jefferson Davis lives in the 1984 Republican platform," his answer made no mention whatsoever of race or slavery. "The platform we had in Dallas, the 1984 Republican platform, all the ideas we supported there—from tax policy, to foreign policy; from individual rights, to neighborhood security—are things that Jefferson Davis believed in."

Thus, the code didn't just provide cover for erstwhile segregationists like Jesse Helms. It also brought into the mainstream a constitutionally and morally corrupt political culture, giving national Republicans a palatable way to pander to racists, quasi-racists, and crypto-racists. The treatment of Klansman-turned-Louisiana-state-representative David Duke at the end of the 1980s illustrates this strategy. Officially and at the national level, George Bush's "kinder, gentler" GOP formally disavowed Duke in 1989, a mere year after it had deployed race-mongering Willie Horton ads against [Democratic presidential candidate] Michael Dukakis.[2] But at the state level, Louisiana Republican committee chair Billy Nungesser quashed a motion to censure Duke—a move encouraged by Republican National Committee chair Lee Atwater on the theory that taking action against Duke would only stoke his image. The real problem, of course, was how the censure might have alienated Duke's constituents.

> *"Republicans [have found] a palatable way to pander to racists, quasi-racists, and crypto-racists."*

But by 1994, this kind of pandering reached a saturation point for the Republicans. That year, GOP candidates in the South cleared out most of the conservative Democrats who had clung, mostly by virtue of incumbency, to what were essentially Republican districts. The remaining southern Democrats, for the most part, depended heavily on black voters and white transplants from the North. Nationally, the GOP's racial wedge strategy risked alienating centrist, tolerant white suburbanites in swing states. And in any case, there were no more racists left to pander to. They were all voting for Republicans anyway.

Part of what made [George W.] Bush's choice of Ashcroft seem so foolish was that Bush and his advisers seemed to have pretty much figured out that racial

---

2. In 1986, Willie Horton, a black man serving a life sentence for murder, was given a forty-eight-hour furlough from prison under an experimental program approved by Massachusetts governor Dukakis. Horton did not return from furlough and was captured several months later after committing rape and murder. The Republican Party used political ads featuring the Horton incident during the 1988 presidential race.

wedgery no longer worked, but Ashcroft obviously hadn't. As governor of Texas, Bush—baby boomer, tolerant guy—learned how to talk to the party's southern base in a political language reminiscent, on racial matters, of Rockefeller Republicanism.[3] Ashcroft seemed to have missed the memo. Whereas Helms, Lott, House Majority Leader Dick Armey, and Senator Phil Gramm of Texas gave rebel-yell interviews to the *Southern Partisan* back in, respectively, 1984, 1984, 1990, and 1983, Ashcroft gave his in 1998, by which time a Republican senator with presidential aspirations should have learned the new etiquette.

Ashcroft, however, quickly learned something else: What it takes these days for a charge of racism to stick, it turns out, is an admission. You have to be a self-identified racist. But even under the old, pre-Bush etiquette (that is, the code), there are no self-identified racist Republicans. There are just southern politicians who believe that Jefferson Davis was an American patriot and that Martin Luther King, Jr., was not. Unfortunately, there aren't any rules—in the Senate confirmation hearings or in American politics generally—for openly challenging the substance of those beliefs. So the debate over John Ashcroft revolved entirely around the question of whether or not he was a good person—that is, whether he bore any personal ill will toward blacks.

> *"There are an awful lot of Republicans who . . . are deliberately indifferent to the cause of civil rights, even on such . . . issues as black disenfranchisement."*

You could see the Democrats struggling with this. "What I couldn't understand," Joe Biden stammered to Ashcroft, "is why, right after this, and this is called to your attention, you just don't say, 'Boom, boom, boom. I should have never got a degree from Bob Jones University; I should have never had this interview.' I mean, as you all know, this place loves contrition. I mean, I've had my share of having to do it. We all make mistakes. But I don't get it. I don't get it." The Republicans did get it. If racism was strictly a question of character, then the debate over Ashcroft would pit their word against . . . nobody's. Because as both Democrats and Republicans seemed to agree, John Ashcroft was a good person. And good people, after all, are not racists. And as both Democrats and Republicans seemed to agree, John Ashcroft was a good person. "I had a good, long talk with John about civil rights laws," President Bush explained after meeting with Ashcroft before the hearings. "This is a good man; he's got a good heart."

Deliberate Indifference

But what's in Ashcroft's heart should never have been the issue. One imagines that there are more than a few Democrats in Congress who, to put it

3. A reference to Nelson Rockefeller, Republican politician who served as New York governor from 1958 to 1973 and as U.S. vice president from 1974 to 1977. Rockefeller was known as a liberal.

plainly, just don't like black people. But there are only a very small number of Democrats in Congress who consistently vote against legislation near and dear to black Americans. Similarly, there are no Republicans in Congress—not John Ashcroft, not Jesse Helms, not anyone—who have gone on *Crossfire* to declare that whites are the master race. But there are an awful lot of Republicans who, like Ashcroft, are deliberately indifferent to the cause of civil rights, even on such nominally nonideological issues as black disenfranchisement. The problem is that the language of race in America is too cramped to adequately describe this brand of indifference. Terms like racist, bigot, and Nazi can't suffice; they imply questions of character and intent that are unanswerable.

In politics a functional definition of racism is ultimately more useful than Bush's what's-in-your-heart definition. The problem, after all, is not that Ashcroft embraces Bob Jones University's racism and anti-Catholicism, but that he was more than willing to benefit—as it must have seemed at the time—from BJU's racism and anti-Catholicism. The problem is not that distorting Ronnie White's record is itself a racist act, but that Ashcroft knew that casting a black judge as "pro-criminal" and "soft" on crime would cater to the worst biases of certain Missouri voters. The problem is not that Ashcroft thinks black people shouldn't be allowed to vote, but that in this day and age he seeks political reward in catering to people—readers and admirers of the *Southern Partisan*, for example—who believe the South should not have lost the Civil War. For a United States senator, pandering to racists is worse than being a racist. For a United States attorney general, it is—or ought to be—unacceptable.

Zionism Is Racism

by Donald Neff

About the author: *Donald Neff is the author of* 50 Years of Israel *and* Fallen Pillars.

You don't need to see racism to recognize it. Unlike pornography, which often is in the eye of the beholder, racism in nations is self-evident. It comes in the form of a constitution, the laws that a nation adopts and the behavior of its citizens toward minorites. Yet the United States failed to recognize racism when the American delegation walked out of the [September 2001] U.N. World Conference Against Racism in sympathy with Israel. Significantly, it was the only country in the world to do so.[1]

What is it that the rest of the world sees when it looks at Israel that Washington doesn't? Other nations note that Israel has no constitution. But it has a body of what are called "Basic Laws" that serve the purpose of a constitution. Among these laws are a number of statutes that enshrine exclusive rights for Jews above all other religions and peoples living in the state.

One such law is the Right of Return, granting any Jew—but no one else—automatic Israeli citizenship. It was passed in 1950 by the Knesset, Israel's parliament, in which there are few non-Jews beyond token members of minor minorities.

In the words of Israel's first prime minister, David Ben-Gurion: "This is not only a Jewish state, where the majority of the inhabitants are Jews, but a state for all Jews, wherever they are, and for every Jew who wants to be here. . . . This right is inherent in being a Jew."

For Jews Only

Another of the Basic Laws is one defining Israel citizenship, passed by the Knesset in 1952. It is the Law of Citizenship, sometimes called the Nationality Law. It set citizenship rules so stringently against non-Jews that many Palestinian residents of Israel (stuck there when Israel captured their land in 1948)

---

1. The United States walked out of the 2001 UN conference to protest other delegations' portrayal of Israel as a racist state.

were denied citizenship even though their families had lived in Palestine for many generations.

In fact, the law was so restrictive against granting citizenship to goyim—a Hebrew term to define all non-Jews—that it caused concern among some Jewish communities outside of Israel. Irving M. Engel, president of the American Jewish Committee, later met with Ben-Gurion and urged him to have the law changed. Engel said he was embarrassed by the restrictive nature of the law, since his organization had crusaded throughout the world for equal treatment of Jews. Now, he added, when Jews got their own country they were discriminating against non-Jews. Ben-Gurion rejected any changes to the Nationality Law.

In the same year, 1952, the Knesset passed the World Zionist Organization–Jewish Agency (Status) Law, which legalized special economic, political and social benefits for Israeli Jews. It gave exclusive rights not to all citizens of Israel but to Israelis of "Jewish nationality," including the right to purchase land. Jewish institutions such as the Jewish National Fund were prohibited by law to sell the land they owned in Israel—some 97 percent—to non-Jews and were enjoined to hold all land "for the whole Jewish people."

Israel is democracy for Jews only.

Racism has many other manifestations in Israel beyond official statutes. Most notable of these prejudicial practices is the ban against Palestinians serving in the Israel Defense Forces. Even though Palestinians make up nearly 20 percent of Israel's population—a larger minority than blacks in America—they are left in the paradoxical position of being denied the basic duty of protecting what is supposedly their country.

Palestinians never gain entry to the higher levels of the Israeli government. There has never been a Palestinian cabinet minister, much less a prime minister or a minister of foreign affairs. Their cities and towns receive nowhere near the financial aid from the central government that their Jewish counterparts receive, nor do their educational and health systems.

> *"Among [Israel's] laws are a number of statutes that enshrine exclusive rights for Jews above all other religions and peoples living in the state."*

Needless to say, the quality of life of the average Palestinian citizen of Israel is far lower than that of Jewish "nationals."

By any definition of racism, Israel qualifies. Its laws and practices define it as exclusionary and for Jews only. While Israel most certainly is a democracy, it is a democracy for Jews only. Goyim are not welcome or accepted as equals.

Palestinians are at best second-class citizens, casualties of a bloody history that left them stranded inside what became Israel. In fact, all non-Jews, whether Palestinians or American Christians, are discouraged from living in Israel. Marriage between a Jew and a non-Jew cannot be performed there. Nor is religious tolerance exactly a hallmark of Israel's democracy. From time to time Israel's

Knesset has passed laws against proselytizing by Christians, decreeing prison terms for both the converted and the converter.

Given this reality, it was hypocritical in the extreme for the U.S. to thumb its nose at the World Conference Against Racism. Surely this country, as one of the world's few true democracies, has a duty to stand up against racism wherever it sees it. Instead it brusquely quit the conference in September [2001] as a show of solidarity with Israel's walkout.

Israeli Apartheid

Secretary of State Colin Powell specifically cited as one of the reasons for the U.S. action the charge by some non-Jewish delegates that "apartheid exists in Israel." How could they say otherwise? Anyone who has ever visited Israel knows that apartheid is alive and well in the Jewish state. What else is the cruel Israeli military occupation and isolation of three million Palestinians—complete with travel permits, checkpoints, "whites-only" neighborhoods and other former trademarks of South Africa?

Powell also complained that delegates regarded "Zionism as racism." But, by its own definition, Zionism is racist. How could it be otherwise? Zionism is specifically for Jews, excluding all others, so by its very nature it is racist. What else could it mean when Jews proudly proclaim Israel is a Jewish state? They mean goyim are not wanted.

What could Secretary of State Powell have been thinking when he uttered these absurd justifications for leaving the conference? Surely it wasn't reality. His charge that Israel was being unfairly discriminated against lost any trace of credibility when not one of the other 163 nations in the world followed Washington's lead, not even such traditional allies as Britain or France.

In fact, after the United States and Israel quit the conference the remaining delegates—i.e., the rest of the world—went on formally to express their concern about the "plight of the Palestinians under foreign occupation." Israel and the United States were left standing alone, in shame.

In the end Powell and his boss, President George W. Bush, sacrificed an important international conference to pander to Zionists and their powerful American political lobby. In the process they besmirched their own reputations and that of their nation.

The Juvenile Justice System Is Not Racist

by Jared Taylor

About the author: *Jared Taylor is president of the New Century Foundation and editor of* American Renaissance, *a conservative monthly newsletter.*

"A black youth is six times more likely to be locked up than a white peer, even when charged with a similar crime and when neither has a record. . . ." So began an April 25 Associated Press news story picked up uncritically by dozens of papers including the *Washington Post* that helped feed a wave of national breast-beating over the unfairness of the juvenile justice system. The story was about a report put out by a San Francisco organization called Building Blocks for Youth, which claimed to "document the cumulative disadvantage of minority youth" in the face of a biased system.

But is the system really that bad? Are black first-time offenders really six times more likely to go to jail than white first-timers charged with the same crimes? Of course not. To its credit, the Building Blocks for Youth report didn't actually say that. To its great discredit the organization has done nothing to dispel an error that perfectly suits its image of prejudiced law-enforcement. The "six times" figure is probably well on its way into the folklore of racial oppression.

What the report says is that during 1993, black juveniles in several states were six times more likely than whites to get locked up in some kind of public facility. It says nothing about what accounts for this six-fold disparity. This finding is vastly different from the claim that made headlines, namely, that blacks are six times more likely than whites to go to jail when they commit the same crimes and have similar records. The mere fact that more blacks than whites are locked up is something criminologists have known for years and does not necessarily suggest justice system bias at all. It may reflect only higher crime rates among blacks.

The media mischief began when this bit of data was bulleted as a "major finding" at the beginning of the report: "When White youth and minority youth were charged with the same offenses, African-American youth with no prior admissions were six times more likely to be incarcerated in public facilities than White youth with the same background." It sure sounds like a stacked deck in court.

"Perhaps the wording in the bullet was misleading," concedes Eileen Poe-Yamagata, one of the report's co-authors. It sure was. It misled nearly every journalist in the country. The *Boston Herald* wrote that "black first-time offenders are six times more likely to be sentenced to prison by juvenile courts than whites." The *Saint Louis Post-Dispatch* led its story with the same shocking finding. The *Chicago Tribune, Cincinnati Enquirer, Cleveland Plain-Dealer* and *Seattle Post-Intelligencer* and plenty of other papers trumpeted the news. William Raspberry agonized over judicial bias in his column. The *Philadelphia Inquirer* wrung its hands over the six times problem in an editorial. It was a startling, incendiary finding and most of the press swallowed it without a gurgle. The *Washington Times* was one of only a handful of newspapers that did not join the pack, baying about racism.

If there really were such strong evidence of racial bias in the justice system it would be newsworthy all right, but that is not what the report found because it is not there to be found. Many studies over the years have determined that when black and white criminals are carefully compared for offense and criminal record, the justice system treats them pretty much the same. As for high rates of incarceration for blacks, compelling evidence from the U.S. government's National Crime Victimization Survey suggests that blacks, juvenile and adult, are overrepresented in jails because they commit more crimes, not because of judicial bias.

> *"Blacks juvenile and adult are overrepresented in jails because they commit more crimes, not because of judicial bias."*

What are the chances Building Blocks for Youth will issue a correction? "We're not really sure at this point," says Miss Poe-Yamagata. "I had noticed in a few of the articles that there could be a need for that, but there hasn't been an official decision on that." Don't count on one anytime soon. Groups like this thrive on charges of racism, not on sober reporting. It is not likely to be much bothered if a disparity in lock-up rates that probably reflects nothing more than high crime rates among blacks has now been twisted into proof that the system is racist.

Charges of Environmental Racism Are Unfounded

by Roger Clegg

About the author: *Roger Clegg is general counsel of the Center for Equal Opportunity and a former deputy in the civil rights and environmental divisions of the U.S. Justice Department.*

The movement for "environmental justice" and against "environmental racism" began in the 1980s. Its premise is that racial minorities, particularly in low-income neighborhoods, suffer disproportionately from pollution.

The data supporting this premise are underwhelming, as Christopher H. Foreman Jr. notes in *The Promise and Peril of Environmental Justice*, his new analysis of the movement. Studies often define "minority community," for example, to include any area where the percentage of nonwhites exceeds the national average, so that a community may be labeled "minority" even though the vast majority of its residents are white. Not only is there little evidence of a correlation between race and the enforcement of pollution laws, but what evidence there is suggests that facilities in minority areas have actually been assessed *higher* penalties than those elsewhere. "Much of the seminal environmental-justice research," Foreman concludes, "has been called into serious question."

The curious thing is that it doesn't seem to matter to believers in environmental justice. As Foreman puts it—under the apt heading "Beyond Evidence"— "formal analysis is to a considerable extent irrelevant to the underlying objectives and gratifications that stir activist and community enthusiasm." Thus, "for many activists, environmental justice is mostly about accountability and political power rather than the more technical issue of environmental risks facing communities.". . .

One venue in which environmental justice . . . found political currency [was] the Clinton administration. In 1994, President [Bill] Clinton signed an executive order declaring that

each Federal agency shall make achieving environmental justice part of its mission by identifying and addressing, as appropriate, disproportionately high and adverse human health or environmental effects of its programs, policies, and activities on minority populations and low-income populations.

As Foreman explains, the Clinton administration embraced environmental justice, not least because "the racial minorities that constituted most of the . . . movement—African Americans, non-Cuban Latinos, and Native Americans— were crucial elements in the Democratic Party's (and President Clinton's) electoral coalition." It was good symbolic politics, even if it had no factual basis. And [in 1998] the Congressional Black Caucus called upon the administration to "strictly enforce its rules making excess pollution in minority areas a civil-rights violation."

The Theory of Disparate Impact

The primary legal tool of environmental justice is the theory of "disparate impact." No one would hesitate to condemn the actual targeting of a neighborhood for pollution *because* it was black. But what [environmental-justice advocates] want to ban is actions that have a disproportionately bad *effect* on minority neighborhoods. The result of disparate-impact theory in employment law, where it began, has been to push employers to adopt racial quotas. And the extension of the doctrine to environmental law now encourages the enforcement of pollution statutes with an eye to race—supposedly the thing that environmental justice opposes. Where pollution is a significant threat to health, it should be addressed no matter what the color of its victims. But color-blindness is not what advocates are after these days.

Earlier [in the twentieth century], the Left characterized the struggle for racial equality as simply one part of its general plan for the redistribution of economic and political power. In more recent years, however, the Left has tried whenever possible to recast each element of its agenda as part of the continuing struggle against racism. The attempt to limit welfare, the war on drugs, and the fight to end racial preferences have all been declared racist. And now pollution is racist, too.

> *"'Much of the seminal environmental-justice research . . . has been called into serious question.'"*

It is not hard to understand why this shift has taken place. The overwhelming majority of Americans oppose racial discrimination. Indeed, the mid-century battles against racial discrimination may be the last time the Left was correct about anything.

It is of course unfair to call businessmen or local zoning officials racist when they are not. But the real victims in this scam are the racial minorities themselves. Crying racism when there is none cheapens the charge and encourages deafness when the claim might be real. Worse, the tactic encourages seeing every misfortune as the product of a racist conspiracy. This is not only false; it saps the self-reliance and personal responsibility essential for anyone to succeed—especially those starting on the lower rungs of the economic ladder.

Racial Quotas and Pollution

When the environmental-justice movement began, it seemed for a short time to promise a division in the Left. "Mainstream environmentalism," writes Foreman, has been "overwhelmingly white and middle-class," more attuned to mountain trails than inner cities. But the leaders of the environmental and civil-rights groups—both against capitalism and in favor of central planning, both populist in theory and elitist in fact—quickly discovered that they could gain by joining forces.

> *"Crying racism when there is none cheapens the charge and encourages deafness when the claim might be real."*

As the child of this union, environmental justice has inherited the worst feature of each parent. The most poisonous item on the civil-rights agenda is racial quotas. And so the environmental-justice movement holds that pollution decisions must be made with reference to race. Foreman notes that at least one advocate has demanded this principle be used to ensure that [the Environmental Protection Agency's] expenditures are racially proportionate—despite the consequent "tendency to hamper the EPA's ability to direct funds where they are most needed in light of other, arguably more compelling, policy criteria, such as public-health impact."

One result is distraction from real health problems. The effect is "particularly insidious" given the fact that those distracted "have even fewer resources, and greater vulnerabilities, than more affluent citizens." Worse, "environmental-justice proponents generally eschew personal behavior (and necessary changes in it) as a primary variable in the health of low-income and minority communities."

A 1994 National Health Interview Survey found that 28 percent of white men smoked, versus 34 percent of black men and 54 percent of Native Americans. Among those at or above the poverty line, 24 percent smoked, while 35 percent of those below it did. Foreman observes that "it might appear mean-spirited rather than helpful to observe that the death of [environmental-justice advocate] Hazel Johnson's husband from lung cancer at age forty-one might have had more to do with his cigarette smoking than with ambient industrial pollution." But it's true. . . .

A Dangerous Distraction

The [environmental-justice] movement doesn't have anything worthwhile to add to the debate about pollution. Not only does it exaggerate the extent to which pollution raises health concerns—something common among environmentalists—but it insists that our environmental and health problems are largely racial, which is simply wrong. The other key premise—that government intervention (rather than free enterprise and personal responsibility) is what poor people need—is wrong, too.

The environmental-justice movement has no support in the empirical data, its legal claims are unsound, and its desired results damage the health and economic possibilities of its intended beneficiaries. Worse, the movement encourages racial paranoia and a victim mentality, distracts attention and energy from valid public-health concerns, and discourages individuals from assuming personal responsibility and adopting a healthy lifestyle. The movement, in short, is a false and dangerous distraction.

The Republican Party Is Not a Racist Institution

by Alvin S. Felzenberg

About the author: *Alvin S. Felzenberg held senior-level positions in George H.W. Bush's administration and served as New Jersey's assistant secretary of state. He is also the editor of* The Keys to a Successful Presidency.

In 1984, in Biloxi, Mississippi, deep in the heart of the old Confederacy, the future Senate majority leader Trent Lott declared that "the spirit of Jefferson Davis" now lives in the Republican party.

It's a mystery quite how the party of Abraham Lincoln, born in the moral outrage of the great northern abolitionists, could become in the minds of some of its most visible modern leaders the party of Davis. To some, Davis's legacy may seem one of support for states' rights. To others, however, he remains a Southern slaveholder, Democrat, and president of a Confederacy born in rebellion and secession.

Or perhaps it's not such a mystery. From their 1854 beginning, the Republicans were the party that fought slavery, imposed Reconstruction, and opposed segregation, while the Democrats were the party of Jim Crow, race baiting, and Dixiecrats. But for many years, "progressive" historians have been telling a story of America's "steady march to liberalism," in which all good comes from Democrats and all evil from Republicans. And not only have Democrats learned this false lesson and claimed an undeserved reputation on race, but even Republicans have absorbed their enemies' lesson—until at last they find themselves claiming Jefferson Davis as one of their own.

A Skewed View on American History

In order to construct their progressive story, these left-leaning historians—Henry Steele Commager, Allen Nevins, Claude G. Bowers, and the Arthur Schlesingers—were forced to pass over innumerable Democratic sins: Andrew Jackson's treatment of native Americans, southern populists' racial demonizing,

Woodrow Wilson's segregationism, William Jennings Bryan's support of the Ku Klux Klan, and Franklin Roosevelt's indifference to anti-lynching legislation.

Simultaneously, they were compelled to ignore the efforts the conservative "stand patters" made to improve race relations. New York boss Roscoe Conkling escorted Mississippi's Hiram Revels, the first black senator, down the aisle to his swearing in when no one else would—but his courage has found few admirers among reform-minded historians. In the 1880s, as a young congressman, Henry Cabot Lodge introduced a voting rights bill—but he's known to history primarily as Woodrow Wilson's antagonist in international relations. "Uncle Joe" Cannon, the tyrannical speaker of the House in the early 1900s, backed every civil rights measure introduced during his long tenure—but he's more famous for liking tariffs and trusts.

> *"From their 1854 beginnings, the Republicans were the party that fought slavery, imposed Reconstruction, and opposed segregation."*

[Republican] Presidents [Ulysses] Grant, [Benjamin] Harrison, [Warren] Harding, and [Calvin] Coolidge tried to outlaw lynching, protect voting rights, and increase tolerance—but all receive "failing" or "below average" grades from historians who disapprove of their economic policies. Textbooks record that [Dwight] Eisenhower sent troops to Little Rock to enforce the Supreme Court's 1954 anti-segregation decision in *Brown* [*vs. Board of Education*]—but always with the caveat that he did so "reluctantly and late." They make less mention of his peaceful desegregation of the nation's capital or his success in passing the first civil rights bill in almost a century despite Democratic efforts to weaken it.

So complete has been the victory of this view of American history that even Republicans turn away from their past: No serious candidate invokes the names of Grant, Harding, Cannon, or Coolidge. Yet African-American activist Frederick Douglass stood up for Grant in his day. His political descendants did the same for other Republicans. If progressive historians had been less willing to relegate race to secondary importance in explaining the past, or if Republicans had proved less apt pupils, the GOP could cite with telling effect a long train of heroes in the fight against racism—beginning with William Lloyd Garrison.

William Lloyd Garrison

In his marvelous new study *All on Fire: William Lloyd Garrison and the Abolition of Slavery*, Henry Mayer has rescued this nineteenth-century abolitionist from common distortions. Historians have typically depicted Garrison as marginal at best and a firebrand fanatic at worst, typical of the abolitionist troublemakers who made more difficult the work of practical politicians like Daniel Webster, Henry Clay, and Stephen Douglas.

But Garrison, in fact, is one of the rare examples of a presumed extremist who proves more practical than the temporizers. All he needed to make his vision a reality was a complete shift in prevailing public opinion—and Garrison did more to bring that shift about than any other figure of his time. Mayer believes Garrison's greatness was his ability to understand that by eschewing both compromise and conventional politics, he could—through logical analysis, agitation, confrontation, and grassroots organizing—move public opinion his way.

Born in 1805, the descendant of indentured servants, Garrison derived his profound religious faith from his mother and his passion for abolition from an early Quaker mentor, Benjamin Lundy. After trying his hand at shoemaking and carpentry, he was apprenticed to a printer at age thirteen—quickly rising to become a professional printer, writer, and newspaper publisher.

But it was in 1829, at age twenty-four, that he first came to broad public notice, delivering a stirring address at Boston's Park Street Church in which he dedicated his life to the fight against slavery. His peroration was reprinted on the masthead of all his future papers: "I am in earnest—I will not equivocate—I will not excuse—I will not retreat a single inch—AND I WILL BE HEARD." In 1831, he launched his newspaper, the *Liberator*, and showed an early capacity to enrage. In 1835, an angry mob would certainly have lynched him had not two burly Irishmen come to his rescue.

But the key to grasping his importance is recognizing how quickly Garrison moved from the fringes of public opinion to the center—or rather, how quickly he moved public opinion, for Garrison never wavered. When, at the July 4, 1854, picnic in

> *"For many years, 'progressive' historians have been telling a story . . . in which all good comes from Democrats and all evil from Republicans."*

Framingham, Massachusettes, Garrison burned a copy of the Constitution, calling it "a covenant with death," few northerners still thought him extreme. Eleven years later, he journeyed to Charleston, South Carolina, as President Lincoln's official representative to observe Union troops retake Fort Sumter.

Garrison knew how to turn events to his advantage. He mockingly asked why—if they thought slavery a moral good—southerners passed laws fining free Negroes who subscribed to the *Liberator.* And as he tormented his opponents, Garrison pressed to make "immediacy" the dominant faction within the abolition movement. He saw parallels between members of the American Colonization Society (who sought to deport freed slaves to Africa) and Jacksonians (who were forcing Cherokees from the Georgia frontier). Both, he said, were trying to deny the universal and biblical promise of the Declaration of Independence to non-whites.

Having succeeded in making "immediacy" the primary objective of most abolitionists, Garrison worked to make it the primary northern response to the secessionist threats issuing from the South. If southerners would leave a Union that resisted the spread of slavery, he and his followers would withdraw from one that compromised with slavery's defenders. Lacking the legal power to abolish slavery outright, northerners could stop sustaining it by themselves breaking away from a flawed covenant.

Rallying Against Slavery

In *All on Fire*, Mayer attributes Garrison's stand to the antinomian, "perfectionist" theology of Charles Grandison Finney (founder of Oberlin College) and the Unitarian "breakawayer," Theodore Parker. Garrison beseeched churchgoers to leave congregations that did not denounce slavery. He also urged his followers not to participate in a political system that delayed immediate change. . . .

While he criticized Lincoln as president for his slowness on slavery, Garrison sensed that the [Civil War] provided the legal means to destroy the practice. When Lincoln finally issued the Emancipation Proclamation [freeing slaves in the South] in 1863, the uncompromising Garrison did not dismiss it as a "fraud" because it exempted territory the Union controlled. He noted instead that it freed the slaves of rebels, offered blacks military protection, and admitted them into the army. Garrison always accepted what he got and pressed on for what he wanted. Through the remainder of the war, he made the case for immediate emancipation of the million slaves still in the border states.

Whatever Lincoln's hesitations, his willingness to engage black troops, nullify fugitive slave laws, and add the Thirteenth Amendment [abolishing slavery] won him Garrison's open support. Lincoln acknowledged the Union's debt to Garrison when he wrote, "The logic and moral power of Garrison and the antislavery people of the country and the army, have done it all." Of Lincoln, Garrison said, "No man ever did so large a business on so small a capital in the service of freedom and humanity." In 1864, for the first time since he burst on the public stage, Garrison issued a political endorsement, editorializing for Lincoln. He remained an active Republican until his death in 1879.

Reaching Out to Southern Blacks

But Garrison found "immediacy" harder to argue in debates over Reconstruction after the war. As Mayer notes in *All on Fire*, these issues did not carry the same "theological burden" as abolition, and they required yet another change in opinion from an exhausted public. Even after slavery had ended, three northern states still denied the vote to freed blacks, and 93 percent of blacks in the North were still disenfranchised.

The Republicans Garrison had joined would spend much of their future debating how to appeal to those they had set free. Mayer describes the problem the party faced at the end of the Civil War:

> This question became one of whether to broaden the party's base with black voters in the South, and risk losing its most conservative and racist voters in the North, or to take a partial victory as a promissory note and expand the party's strength on the basis of other issues.

Until the end of Ulysses S. Grant's presidency, the Republicans tried the first approach. Reaching out to southern blacks was a key component of the Reconstruction plans of Senator Charles Sumner, Representative Thaddeus Stevens, and other "Radical Republicans." It was central in their battle with President Andrew Johnson. With one eye fixed on continued GOP majorities and another on improving the condition of blacks, the Radicals gave southern states a choice: Either grant the franchise to their former slaves or have their congressional delegations reduced.

The "reconstructed states" responded by restricting the rights of emancipated slaves. Terrorist bands intimidated those who attempted to vote. Former Confederate politicians and officers were elected to Congress. (The Radicals refused to seat them.) After Johnson vetoed civil rights laws and refused to enforce the rights of blacks, Congress imposed its own reconstruction plan by legislation, constitutional amendment, and, ultimately, impeachment.

Radicals and their black supporters in the South expected the stalemate between Congress and the president to end with Ulysses S. Grant's election in 1868. Grant had allowed two hundred thousand liberated slaves into Union combat forces (part of his strategy to win the war by "attrition") and had sided with the Radicals in their rift with Johnson.

> *"[Republican abolitionist] Garrison beseeched churchgoers to leave congregations that did not denounce slavery."*

Once in office, Grant repeatedly sent troops to southern polling places to assure African Americans the right to vote. He relentlessly pursued the fledgling Ku Klux Klan and denounced color prejudice as "senseless." He invoked market-based justifications for his attempt to acquire the Dominican Republic, arguing that blacks might use their ability to sell their labor at higher wages there as leverage to persuade southern employers to pay them higher wages.

But Grant nonetheless failed, primarily because it was impossible for him to achieve both sectional reconciliation and equal justice for blacks. Grant described how his efforts on behalf of former slaves in the South eroded his base of support elsewhere:

> The whole public are tired out with these annual, autumnal outbreaks in the South, and there is so much unwholesome lying done by the press and people in regard to the cause and extent of these breaches of the peace that the great majority were ready now to condemn any interference on the part of the Government.

The 1876 election of "His Fraudulency," Rutherford B. Hayes, brought to an end Republican efforts to protect blacks. Though he lost the popular vote, Hayes became president when electors in three southern states shifted their votes in exchange for his promise to withdraw all remaining federal troops from the South.

Political Realignments

For the next eighty years, Republicans turned to Mayer's "other issues": sound money, tariffs, economic development, civil service, trust busting, and taxes. Some of these may have slowed the economic advance of former slaves. Civil service reform, for instance—a favorite cause among progressive historians—ended the patronage Republicans had used to help blacks. Through his political alliance with Booker T. Washington, Theodore Roosevelt appointed blacks to federal posts over local objections.

But having acquiesced in the disenfranchisement of their southern black supporters, Republicans sought to make their party competitive in the region by attracting whites. It didn't work—and Frederick Douglass explained why: "If anything, the South became, with every concession made by the Republicans, . . . more Democratic. There never was yet, and there never will be, an instance of permanent success where a party abandons its righteous principles to win favor of the opposing party."

For their part, the Democrats, from Andrew Johnson's presidency to Lyndon Johnson's, sought to reassemble the Jacksonian coalition of northern machines and southern segregationists. In 1924, Franklin Roosevelt advised Democrats to raise only issues of importance to the entire nation—which meant that they should stay away from the question of integration. [Harry S.] Truman did desegregate the armed forces, and [John F.] Kennedy enforced court orders to integrate southern state universities. Yet all three looked upon civil rights advocates primarily as interests to be managed rather than integral parts of their electoral coalitions.

Buoyed by a changed public opinion, produced by Garrison's spiritual heirs who marched with Martin Luther King Jr., Lyndon Johnson brought an end to Jim Crow and made voting rights a reality for millions of African Americans. His deeds, plus his Republican opponent Barry Goldwater's opposition to the 1964 civil rights bill, hastened a realignment of the two parties with African Americans voting for the Democrats and southern whites for the Republicans. Where [Richard] Nixon had still carried 32 percent of the African-American vote in 1960, Goldwater's share dropped to 6 percent, and no GOP presidential standard bearer has fared much better since: Nixon, 1968: 12 percent; Nixon, 1972: 13 percent; [Gerald] Ford, 1976: 15 percent; [Ronald] Reagan, 1980: 10 percent; Reagan, 1984: 13 percent; [George] Bush, 1988: 18 percent; Bush, 1992: 11 percent; [Bob] Dole, 1996: 12 percent.

Collective Amnesia

Several myths arose after the 1964 election that cloud impressions minorities have of the Republicans' past—and form the image many Republicans hold of themselves.

One myth is that Goldwater's anti-civil rights vote was rooted in racism. More a libertarian than anything else, Goldwater opposed sections of the bill that denied private businesses the right to deny service to any person for any reason. In his home state of Arizona, Goldwater was known as an advocate of integration. His commitment to "voluntary association" blinded him to the reality that where Rosa Parks could sit on a bus was prescribed by state law.

Another myth is that Goldwater represented his entire party's position on civil rights. Twenty-seven of the thirty-one other Republican senators supported the bill. Twenty-one Democrats voted against it, among them Sam Ervin (star of the Watergate hearings), J. William Fulbright (an early Vietnam war skeptic), Robert Byrd (the "constitutional authority" of the Clinton impeachment), and Albert Gore [father of former vice president Al Gore]. Such "right wing Neanderthals" as Karl Mundt, Carl Curtis, and Roman Hruska voted for it. The most eloquent speech came from Republican minority leader Everett Dirksen, quoting Victor Hugo: "Nothing is so powerful as an idea whose time has come."

The story was similar in the House. Understandably, liberal historians and activists have downplayed the role of Republicans in breaking Democratic filibusters and securing final passage. Less understandable is what sustains collective amnesia among Republicans. When he ascended in 1994, the first Republican speaker of the House in over forty years, Newt Gingrich said: "No Republican here should kid themselves about it. The greatest leaders in fighting for an integrated America in the twentieth century were in the Democratic party. The fact is, it was the liberal wing of the Democratic party that ended segregation."

> *"Reaching out to southern blacks was a key component of the Reconstruction plans of . . . 'Radical Republicans.'"*

None of Gingrich's consistent efforts on behalf of the nation's capital, its public schools, scholarships for poor children, and Habitat for Humanity could change those impressions. Other Republican officials, apologizing for their party's having been on the "wrong side" of the issue when it wasn't, have fared no better. And some Republican conservatives have even tried to claim the mantle of George Wallace, a man who was neither a Republican nor a conservative. In a 1968 straw poll, even the "country-club" Republican Nelson Rockefeller out-polled Wallace among conservatives, 43 percent to 23 percent. (Given a choice only between two big-spending liberals, they chose the one who did not apply racial tests—proving conservatives of the time were neither racist nor stupid.)

By failing to come to terms with its true history on race, the modern Republican party remains saddled with the worst of all worlds and bereft of a policy. On some occasions, Republicans have acted as though they accepted Democratic caricatures of themselves as "uncaring bigots." And as if to prove they are not, they let stand programs they believe both wrong and unsuccessful, like bilingual education, affirmative action, and racial set asides.

The rest of the time, with the exception of welfare reform and flirtations with "negative income taxes," "enterprise zones," and "school choice," Republicans offer few alternatives to Democratic programs. Republicans show signs of disappointment and even hurt at their opponents' failure to credit them at least for their altruism. But when will such truly Republican notions as community renewal legislation, school choice, and authorization for faith-based entities to compete for public funds—all the profoundly conservative plans that offer real hope to the African-American community—ever receive from GOP leadership the same priority as tax cuts, Social Security, and missile defense?

Much as they insist on their commitment to "inclusion," the Republicans will never recruit minority voters back to what was their natural home until the party stops believing the "progressive" view that has denied the long history of Democratic vices and Republican virtues on black-white relations. Only then can the party return to its original ideas of equality of opportunity and equality before the law. Only then can the party cease to oscillate between behaving as a shamed clone of the Democrats on issues of race, and simply ignoring blacks as a Democratic interest group.

An accurate rendering of our history can teach modern Republicans a lesson in practical politics, and it can teach them a lesson as well in moral leadership. Sometimes the two do come together—and William Lloyd Garrison remains the best person to remind us of that.

Zionism Is Not Racism

by Michael Melchior

About the author: *Michael Melchior is a rabbi and a deputy foreign minister of the state of Israel.*

Editor's Note: The following statement was delivered, in slightly different form, before the UN World Conference Against Racism in Durban, South Africa, on September 3, 2001. The Israeli delegation walked out of the conference to protest several nations' allegations that Zionism—the reestablishment of a Jewish homeland in Israel—was a form of racism.

Why, when the world was created, did God create just one man, Adam, and one woman, Eve? The Rabbis answered: so that all humankind would come from a single union, to teach us that we are all brothers and sisters.

This conference [the September 2001 UN World Conference Against Racism] was dedicated to that simple proposition. We, all of us, have a common lineage and are all, irrespective of race, religion, or gender, created in the divine image. Indeed, this single idea, unknown to all other ancient civilizations, may be the greatest gift that the Jewish people has given to the world, the recognition of the equality and dignity of every human being.

The foremost right that follows from this principle is the right to be free, not to be a slave. It is imperative that the international community address and duly acknowledge—already far, far too late—the magnitude of the tragedy of slavery.

Suffering and Moral Responsibility

The horror of slavery is profoundly engraved in the experience of the Jewish people—a people formed in slavery. For hundreds of years, the children of Israel were enslaved in Egypt, until, as the book of Exodus recounts, the call: "Let my people go" heralded the first national liberation movement in history, and the model for every liberation that was to follow.

The Jewish response to slavery was remarkable. Rather than forget or sublimate the suffering of slavery, Jewish tradition insisted that every Jew must remember and relive it. And to this day, on Passover, every Jewish family reenacts the experience of slavery, eats the bread of affliction, and appreciates once again the taste of freedom. Through the ages of our exile this psychodrama has had a profound impact on the Jewish psyche: making sure that every child born into comfort knows the pain of oppression, and every child born into oppression knows the hope of redemption.

But remembrance of our suffering as slaves has a more important function—to remind ourselves of our moral obligations. The experience of oppression brings no privilege, but rather responsibility. We have a responsibility to protect the weak, the widow, the orphan, and the stranger, because, as the Bible says: "You yourselves were strangers in the land of Egypt." Even God, in the first and most fundamental of the ten commandments, identifies Himself not as "Creator of the World," or "Splitter of the Red Sea," but as "the One who freed you from slavery."

> *"In every country in which they have lived, Jews have been in the forefront of the battle for human rights and freedom from oppression."*

And indeed in every country in which they have lived, Jews have been in the forefront of the battle for human rights and freedom from oppression. The same urge for national liberation that led to the Exodus, and that led to the Zionist dream that Jews could live in freedom in their land, was bound up intrinsically with the belief that not just one people, but all peoples, must be free. It was this conviction that Theodor Herzl, the founder of the Zionist movement, expressed in his book, *Altneuland*, as early as 1902:

> There is still one problem of racial misfortune unsolved. The depths of that problem only a Jew can comprehend. I refer to the problem of the Blacks. Just call to mind all those terrible episodes of the slave trade, of human beings who merely because they were black were stolen like cattle, taken prisoners, captured and sold. Their children grew up in strange lands, the objects of contempt and hostility because their complexions were different. I am not ashamed to say, though I may expose myself to ridicule for saying so, that once I have witnessed the redemption of Israel, my people, I wish to assist the redemption of the Black people.

As Herzl understood, remembrance of slavery is integral to the Jewish experience. A Jew cannot be truly free if he or she does not have compassion for those who are enslaved.

Antisemitism and the Holocaust

If slavery is one form of racist atrocity, antisemitism is another. And by antisemitism, let us be clear; we mean the hatred of Jews. The word "antisemitism" was deliberately coined in 1879 by Wilhelm Marr, an anti-Jewish racist in Germany, to replace the term *judenhass*, Jew-hatred, which had gone out of favor.

It has always been used to describe hatred and discrimination directed at Jews. Attempts to eradicate the plain meaning of the word are not only antisemitic; indeed they are antisemantic.

Those uncomfortable with recognizing the existence of antisemitism not only try to redefine the term; they try to deny that it is different from any other form of discrimination. But it is a unique form of hatred. It is directed at those of particular birth, irrespective of their faith, and those of particular faith, irrespective of their birth. It is the oldest and most persistent form of group hatred. In [the twentieth] century this ultimate hatred . . . led to the ultimate crime, the Holocaust.

But antisemitism goes far beyond hatred of Jews. It has arisen where Jews have never lived, and survives where only Jewish cemeteries remain. And while Jews may be the first to suffer from its influence, they have rarely been the last.

Antisemitism reveals the inner corruption of a society, because at its root it is fueled by a rejection of the humane and moral values the Jewish people bequeathed to the world. As Anne Frank, the Jewish schoolgirl in hiding from the Nazis in occupied Amsterdam, wrote in her *Diary:* "If we bear all this suffering and if there are still Jews left, when it is over, then Jews, instead of being doomed, will be held up as an example. Who knows, it might even be our religion from which the world and all peoples learn good, and for that reason only do we now suffer."

Anne Frank was murdered by the Nazis in Bergen-Belsen for being a Jew, just one of over one million Jewish children to be killed in the Holocaust.

Those who cannot bring themselves to recognize the unique evil of antisemitism similarly cannot accept the stark fact of the Holocaust, the first systematic attempt to destroy an entire people. The past decade has witnessed an alarming increase in attempts to deny the simple fact of this atrocity, at the very time that the Holocaust is passing from living memory into history. After wiping out six million Jewish lives, there are those who would wipe out their deaths. At this conference, too, we have witnessed a vile attempt to generalize and pluralize the word "Holocaust," and to empty it of its meaning as a reference to a specific historic event with a clear and vital message for all humanity.

Could there be anything worse than to brutally, systematically annihilate a people; to take the proud Jews of Vilna, Warsaw, Minsk, Lodz; to burn their holy books; to steal their dignity, their freedom, their hair, their teeth; to turn them into numbers, into slaves, into the ashes of Auschwitz, Treblinka, Majdanek, and Dachau? Could anything be worse than this?

> *"[Zionism] is like the liberation movements of Africa and Asia, the national liberation movement of the Jewish people."*

And the answer is yes, there is something even worse: to do such a thing, and then to deny it, to trivialize it, to take from the mourners, the children, and the grandchildren the legitimacy of their grief, and from all humanity the urgent lesson that might stop it from happening again.

The Zionist Dream

The 20th century that witnessed the atrocities of the Holocaust also witnessed the fulfillment of the Zionist dream: the reestablishment of a Jewish state in Israel's historic land. For Zionism is quite simply that—the national movement of the Jewish people, based on an unbroken connection, going back some 4,000 years, between the People of the Book and the Land of the Bible. It is like the liberation movements of Africa and Asia, the national liberation movement of the Jewish people.

And it is a movement of which other national liberation movements can be justly proud. It has striven continuously to establish a society that reflects the highest ideals of democracy and justice for all its inhabitants, in which Jews and Arabs can live together, in which women and men have equal rights, in which there is freedom of thought, of expression, and in which all have access to the judicial process to ensure that these rights are protected.

> *"The conflict between Israel and its Palestinian neighbors is not racial. . . . It is political and territorial."*

The aspiration to build such a society was enshrined from the outset in Israel's Declaration of Independence: "The State of Israel . . . will foster the development of the country for the benefit of all its inhabitants; it will ensure complete equality of social and political rights to all its inhabitants, irrespective of creed, race or gender; it will guarantee freedom of religion, conscience, language, education and culture."

It is a tall task. It is a constant struggle. And we do not always succeed. But, even in the face of the open hostility of its neighbors and continued threats to its existence, there are few countries that have made such efforts to realize such a vision. Few countries of Israel's age and size have welcomed immigrants from over 100 countries, of all colors and tongues, sent medical aid and disaster relief to alleviate human tragedy wherever it strikes, maintained a free press, including the freest Arabic press anywhere in the Middle East.

And yet those who cannot bring themselves to say the words, "the Holocaust," or to recognize antisemitism for the evil that it is, would have us condemn the "racist practices of Zionism." Did any one of those Arab states that conceived this obscenity stop for one moment to consider its own record? Or to think, for that matter, of the situation of the Jews and other minorities in all the Arab countries?

These states would have us believe that they are anti-Zionist, not antisemitic, but again and again this lie is disproved. What are the despicable caricatures of Jews that fill the Arab press and are being circulated at this conference? What are the vicious libels so freely invented and disseminated by our enemies—about the use of poison gas, or depleted uranium bullets, or injecting babies with the AIDS virus—if not the reincarnation of age-old antisemitic canards?

Chapter 2

The Truth About Anti-Zionism

To criticize policies of the government of Israel—or of any country—is legitimate, even vital; indeed, as Israel is a democratic state, many Israelis do just that. But there is a profound difference between criticizing a country and denying its right to exist. Anti-Zionism, the denial of the Jews' basic right to a home, is nothing but antisemitism, pure and simple. As Dr. Martin Luther King, Jr. wrote:

> You declare, my friend, that you do not hate the Jews, you are merely "anti-Zionist." And I say, let the truth ring forth from the high mountain tops. Let it echo through the valleys of God's green earth: When people criticize Zionism they mean Jews . . . Zionism is nothing less than the dream and ideal of the Jewish people returning to live in their own land. . . . And what is anti-Zionism? It is the denial to the Jew of the fundamental right that we justly claim for the people of Africa and freely accord to all other nations of the globe. It is discrimination against Jews because they are Jews. In short it is antisemitism.

The venal hatred of Jews that has taken the form of anti-Zionism and that has surfaced at this conference is, however, different in one crucial way from the antisemitism of the past. Today, it is being deliberately propagated and manipulated for political ends. Children are not born as racists; racism is a result of lack of education and political manipulation. And today, generations of Palestinian children are being deliberately and systematically indoctrinated, with textbooks stained with blood libels and children's television programs dripping with hatred. This high-risk strategy is bound to fail, but it will exact a heavy price.

The conflict between Israel and its Palestinian neighbors is not racial and has no place at this conference. It is political and territorial. As such, it can and should be resolved to end the suffering and bring peace and security to the Israeli and Palestinian peoples. The path towards such a resolution is clear: an immediate cessation of violence and terror and a return to negotiations as recommended by the Mitchell Committee Report, which both parties have accepted. The outrageous and manic accusations we have heard here are attempts to turn a political issue into a racial one, with almost no hope of resolution.

"Vicious libels . . . will do nothing to prevent more Israeli and Palestinian mothers and fathers bringing their young ones to their graves."

[In the year 2000], at Camp David, the Israeli government demonstrated its deep commitment to peace by offering its Palestinian neighbors far-reaching compromises. These compromises, you will recall, were applauded by the entire international community. But the Palestinians did not accept these proposals, nor did they put forward any compromise proposals of their own. To Israel's deep dismay, they responded with a wave of violence. [During 2001], this violence has escalated into protracted and inhuman attacks on the Israeli civilian population, forcing Israel to assume a role it abhors, defending its citizens by military means we had hoped and prayed would have been relegated to the past.

I will not refer here at length to the disappointing statement we have heard from the head of the Palestinian Authority. Rather than utilize this vital forum to inspire his own people, and the people of the world, to seek peace, honor, and harmony, he chose to use this podium to incite bitterness and hatred. Another missed opportunity by the leader of the Palestinian people.

My own cousins, two little daughters and their brother, lost their legs only a few weeks ago in a terrorist attack on a bus carrying children to school. Many Palestinian children have likewise been wounded for life. The vicious libels, the delegitimization and dehumanization we have heard at this conference will do nothing to prevent more Israeli and Palestinian mothers and fathers bringing their young ones to their graves.

Sacrificing Humanity's Highest Values

But here today, something greater even than peace in the Middle East is being sacrificed—the highest values of humanity. Racism, in all its forms, is one of the most widespread and pernicious evils, depriving millions of hope and fundamental rights. It might have been hoped that this first conference of the 21st century would have taken up the challenge of, if not eradicating racism, at least disarming it. But instead, humanity is being sacrificed to a political agenda. Barely a decade after the UN repealed the infamous "Zionism is Racism" resolution, which Secretary-General Kofi Annan described, with characteristic understatement, as a "low point" in the history of the United Nations, a group of states for whom the terms "racism," "discrimination," and even "human rights" simply do not appear in their domestic lexicon, have hijacked this conference and plunged us into even greater depths.

Can there be a greater irony than the fact that a conference convened to combat the scourge of racism should give rise to the most racist declaration in a major international organization since the Second World War?

Despite the vicious antisemitism we have heard here, I do not fear for the Jewish people, who have learned to be resilient and to hold fast to their faith.

Despite the virulent incitement against my country, I do not fear for Israel, which has the strength not just of courage, but also of conviction.

But I do fear, deeply, for the victims of racism, for the slaves, the disenfranchised, the oppressed, the inexplicably hated, the impoverished, the despised, the millions who turn their eyes to this hall in the frail hope that it may address their suffering, who see instead that a blind and venal hatred of the Jews has turned their hopes into a farce. For them I fear.

We are here as representatives of states, and states by their nature have political interests and agendas. But we are also human beings, all of us brothers and sisters created in the divine image. And in those quiet moments when we recognize our common humanity and look into our souls, let us consider what we came here to do—and what we have in fact done.

We came to learn from our history, but we find it being buried to hide its lesson.

We came to communicate in the language of humanity, but we hear its vocabulary twisted beyond all comprehension.

We came out of respect for the sacred values entrusted to us, but we see them here perverted for political ends.

And ultimately, we came to serve the victims of racism, but we have witnessed yet another atrocity committed in their name.

Chapter 3

Should Affirmative Action Be Abolished?

Affirmative Action in Education: An Overview

by Kenneth Jost

About the author: *Kenneth Jost is a staff writer for the* CQ Researcher, *a weekly report on current issues.*

Jennifer Gratz wanted to go to the University of Michigan's flagship Ann Arbor campus as soon as she began thinking about college. "It's the best school in Michigan to go to," she explains.

The white suburban teenager's dream turned to disappointment in April 1995, however, when the university told her that even though she was "well qualified," she had been rejected for one of the nearly 4,000 slots in the incoming freshman class.

Gratz was convinced something was wrong. "I knew that the University of Michigan was giving preference to minorities," she says today. "If you give extra points for being of a particular race, then you're not giving applicants an equal opportunity."

A Long-Simmering Conflict

Gratz, now 24, has a degree from Michigan's less prestigious Dearborn campus and a job in San Diego. She is also the lead plaintiff in a lawsuit that is shaping up as a decisive battle in the long-simmering conflict over racial preferences in college admissions.

On the opposite side of Gratz's federal court lawsuit is Lee Bollinger, Michigan's highly respected president and a staunch advocate of race-conscious admissions policies.

"Racial and ethnic diversity is one part of the core liberal educational goal," Bollinger says. "People have different educational experiences when they grow up as an African-American, Hispanic or white."

Gratz won a partial victory in December 2000 when a federal judge agreed that the university's admissions system in 1995 was illegal. But the ruling came

Kenneth Jost, "Affirmative Action," *CQ Researcher*, vol. 11, September 21, 2001, pp. 739–40. Copyright © 2001 by Congressional Quarterly, Inc. Reproduced by permission.

too late to help her, and Judge Patrick Duggan went on to rule that the revised system the university adopted in 1998 passed constitutional muster.

Some three months later, however, another federal judge ruled in a separate case that the admissions system currently used at the university's law school is illegal. Judge Bernard Friedman said the law school's admissions policies were "practically indistinguishable from a quota system."

The two cases—*Gratz v. Bollinger* and *Grutter v. Bollinger*—are now set to be argued together [in late 2001] before the federal appeals court in Cincinnati. And opposing lawyers and many legal observers expect the two cases to reach the Supreme Court in a potentially decisive showdown. "One of these cases could well end up in the Supreme Court," says Elizabeth Barry, the university's associate vice president and deputy general counsel, who is co-ordinating the defense of the two suits.[1]

> *"Traditional civil rights groups say racial admissions policies are essential to ensure racial and ethnic diversity at the nation's elite universities."*

"We hope the Supreme Court resolves this issue relatively soon," says Michael Rosman, attorney for the Center for Individual Rights in Washington, which represents plaintiffs in both cases. "It is fair to say that there is some uncertainty in the law in this area."

A Fractured Ruling

The legal uncertainty stems from the long time span . . . since the Supreme Court's only previous full-scale ruling on race-based admissions policies: the famous *Bakke* decision. In that fractured ruling, *University of California Regents v. Bakke*, the high court in 1978 ruled that fixed racial quotas were illegal but allowed the use of race as one factor in college admissions.

Race-based admissions policies are widespread in U.S. higher education today—"well accepted and entrenched," according to Sheldon Steinbach, general counsel of the pro-affirmative action American Council on Education.

Roger Clegg, general counsel of the Center for Equal Opportunity, which opposes racial preferences, agrees with Steinbach but from a different perspective. "Evidence is overwhelming that racial and ethnic discrimination occurs frequently in public college and university admissions." Clegg says.

Higher-education organizations and traditional civil rights groups say racial admissions policies are essential to ensure racial and ethnic diversity at the nation's elite universities—including the most selective state schools, such as Michigan's Ann Arbor campus. "The overwhelming majority of students who apply to highly selective institutions are still white," says Theodore Shaw, asso-

---

1. The federal appeals court upheld the lower court's ruling in *Grutter*, but delayed making a ruling in the *Gratz* case. In 2003, both cases were appealed to the Supreme Court.

ciate director-counsel of the NAACPA [National Association for the Advancement of Colored People] Legal Defense Fund, which represents minority students who intervened in the two cases. "If we are not conscious of selecting minority students, they're not going to be there."

Opponents, however, say racial preferences are wrong in terms of law and social policy. "It's immoral. It's illegal. It stigmatizes the beneficiary. It encourages hypocrisy. It lowers standards. It encourages the use of stereotypes," Clegg says. "There are all kinds of social costs, and we don't think the benefits outweigh those costs."

Increasing Minority Enrollment

The race-based admissions policies now in use around the country evolved gradually since the passage of federal civil rights legislation in the mid-1960s. By 1970, the phrase "affirmative action" had become common usage to describe efforts to increase the number of African-Americans (and, later, Hispanics) in U.S. workplaces and on college campuses. Since then, the proportions of African-Americans and Hispanics on college campuses have increased, though they are still underrepresented in terms of their respective proportions in the U.S. population.

Michigan's efforts range from uncontroversial minority-outreach programs to an admissions system that explicitly takes an applicant's race or ethnicity into account in deciding whether to accept or reject the applicant. The system formerly used by the undergraduate College of Literature, Science and the Arts had separate grids for white and minority applicants. The current system uses a numerical rating that includes a 20-point bonus (out of a total possible score of 150) for "underrepresented minorities"—African-Americans, Hispanics and Native Americans (but not Asian-Americans). The law school's system—devised in 1992—is aimed at producing a minority enrollment of about 10 percent to 12 percent of the entering class.

Critics of racial preferences say they are not opposed to affirmative action. "Certainly there are some positive aspects to affirmative action," Rosman says, citing increased recruitment of minorities and reassessment by colleges of criteria for evaluating applicants. But, he adds, "To the extent that it suggests that they have carte blanche to discriminate between people on the basis of race, it's not a good thing."

Higher-education officials respond that they should have discretion to explicitly consider race—along with a host of other factors—to ensure a fully representative student body and provide the best learning environment for an increasingly multicultural nation and world. "Having a diverse student body contributes to the educational process and is necessary in the 21st-century global economy," Steinbach says.

Affirmative Action Is a Threat to Equality

by Ward Connerly

About the author: *Ward Connerly is chairman of the American Civil Rights Institute.*

On July 20, 1995, the Regents of the University of California (UC) eliminated the consideration of race, gender, color, ethnicity, and national origin in the admissions, contracting, and employment activities of the university. Thus, UC became the first public institution in America to confront its system of preferential policies. With that action, the Regents began a new era of civil rights reform, a new way of looking at race in America, and a return to a well-established American ideal.

Coming on the heels of the UC Regents' action was the overwhelming (54 percent to 46 percent) passage of the California Civil Rights Initiative (Proposition 209) by the voters of California. Proposition 209, approved on November 5, 1996, provided that "the state shall not discriminate against, or grant preferential treatment to, any individual or group, on the basis of race, sex, color, ethnicity or national origin, in the operation of public employment, public education or public contracting."

A Remarkable Victory

On November 3, 1998, the electorate of the state of Washington, in an election that can only be described as remarkable, approved Initiative 200 (I-200), a clone of California's Proposition 209. I-200 was approved by a margin of 58 percent to 42 percent. What made the victory remarkable and, indeed, revealing about the matter of race in America was the number of obstacles that had to be overcome to achieve the result.

I-200 was opposed by the popular Democratic governor of Washington, the Washington Democratic Party, the largest employers in Washington—Boeing, Microsoft, U.S. Bank, Weyerhaeuser, Eddie Bauer Company—and those who lay claim to being civil rights champions: the Urban League, the NAACP [National Association for the Advancement of Colored People], Jesse Jackson, [California representative] Maxine Waters, and others. The initiative was also opposed by virtually every newspaper in Washington, particularly the *Seattle Times*, whose publisher donated full-page ads worth more than $200,000 to defeat the measure. Vice President Al Gore made four trips to Washington to raise funds and speak out against I-200.

In this election, the voters also reelected freshman Democrat Patty Murray to the U.S. Senate, ousted two-term Republican congressman Rick White, stripped control of both houses of the Washington state legislature from Republicans, defeated a measure that would have banned partial-birth abortions, and approved a measure dramatically increasing the minimum wage.

In the face of these events, I-200 received the nod from 80 percent of Republicans, 62 percent of independents, 41 percent of Democrats, 54 percent of labor, and the majority of women (despite a campaign barrage aimed at convincing women that the initiative would adversely affect their best interests).

> *"[Affirmative action] is a direct threat to the culture of equality that defines the character of the nation."*

The exit polls tell the story: the people of Washington had decided that the time had come to end race-based preferences. Less than 15 percent of the electorate believed that it was still appropriate to compensate black people for past wrongs. The overwhelming majority of the electorate concluded that all residents of the state should be treated equally: no discrimination and no preferences.

The Culture of Equality

Why did the voters of Washington ignore the advice of politically correct big corporations, politicians, the media, and race advocates, who hid behind the moral fig leaves of "diversity" and "inclusion," and end the system of preferences and de facto quotas that has come to define affirmative action?

The answer is simple. There is a deeply rooted culture of equality in America that transcends political correctness, partisanship, and ideology. We can trace this culture back to the Declaration of Independence: "We hold these truths to be self-evident, that all men are created equal."

This culture of equality was underscored by Abraham Lincoln: "Four score and seven years ago, our fathers brought forth on this continent a new nation conceived in liberty and dedicated to the proposition that all men are created equal." When Martin Luther King Jr. led the nation through the tumultuous civil rights era, beginning with the public bus boycott in Montgomery [Alabama] in 1955, he invoked that culture of equality in calling on America to "live out the true meaning of your creed." The principle of equality has been embraced by liberal Democrats and conservative Republicans alike, from Lyndon Johnson to Ronald Reagan.

The debate about affirmative action preferences is fundamentally about the rights and responsibilities of American citizenship. It is about whether we will have a system of government and a social system in which we see each other as equals. Although often lost in the rhetorical clamor about its benefits, race-based affirmative action as a concept is, at its core, a challenge to the relationship between individuals and their government. It is a direct threat to the culture of equality that defines the character of the nation.

Two Essential Questions

Those who support affirmative action programs contend that such programs are necessary to provide equal opportunity for women and minorities. The argument is routinely advanced that without affirmative action women and minorities will be subject to the vagaries of the "good old boys network" and will be denied the opportunity of full participation in American life. But when you strip away all the rhetoric about "leveling the playing field" and "building diversity," preferential policies reduce themselves to two essential questions.

First, are white males entitled to the same assertion of civil rights and equal treatment under the law as women and minorities? Second, how much longer is the nation going to maintain policies that presume that American-born black people are mentally inferior and incapable of competing head-to-head with other people, except in athletics and entertainment? We cannot resolve the issue of race in America without coming to terms with these two questions. And we certainly cannot reconcile the conflicts about affirmative action preferences without answering these questions. More than anything else, however, the debate about race-based preferences has focused the nation's attention on the politics of race.

"How much longer is the nation going to maintain policies that presume that American-born black people are mentally inferior?"

The affirmative action debates in California and Washington should convince us that we cannot settle the matter of race in America without settling the issue of affirmative action. But when we resolve the issue of affirmative action, we will be laying the foundation for the kind of race relations that the nation needs in order to live out the true meaning of its creed: one nation, indivisible.

Multicultural Groupthink

American society was conceived and has been nurtured through the years as a society of individuals. At the center of our society is the concept that we are all a minority of one. Obviously, policies that herd the American people into groups, or political enclaves, are in direct conflict with the spirit of individualism that characterizes the nation. The phrase "people of color" has come to describe the way in which race and ethnicity are being politicized in America. Implicit in this phrase is the coalescing of minorities into a coalition or political caucus, which, together with white women, constitutes a power base of sufficient magnitude to preserve race- and gender-based preferences and to achieve other political benefits for the coalition.

Every day, in every region and hamlet of America, we are witnessing the deterioration of American individualism and the ascension of political group thinking, of which preferential policies are the most visible manifestation. How does this form of identity politics play out in the broader societal context? We don't have to look far to find evidence of how individuals identity with their group as opposed to reacting to issues as individuals. The O. J. Simpson verdict illustrated the profound difference between black and white groups in their perception of the American criminal justice system. Welfare reform was another example of differences between black and white. According to some polls, more than 70 percent of black people initially opposed welfare reform, while a similar percentage of white people favored reform. Finally, black people support affirmative action preferences by about the same percentage as white people oppose them (more than 65 percent in most public opinion polls).

Preferences Defeat Our Culture of Equality

The result of the 1960s civil rights movement should have been the promise of equal treatment under the law for all Americans. Instead, the result has been a presumption that the very term *civil rights* is synonymous with the rights of black people. In America, we are engaged in an exciting adventure, an adventure that is unrivaled elsewhere in the world. Can we take people from around the globe, who come from different cultures, who have different religious beliefs, who embrace different political ideologies, and who are all colors of the rainbow, and assimilate their differences into a common culture and national identity?

When Thomas Jefferson and the other founders laid out this adventure, they gave their new nation a moral blueprint to make the adventure a success. The centerpiece of that blueprint is our system of moral principles. Moral principles do not change with the seasons. That is precisely why the founders proclaimed that certain truths are "self-evident" and "endowed by our Creator." They are not meant to change or to be bargained away. Our inalienable rights are the centerpiece of that moral system, and the principle of equality is central to our system of rights.

But what can the average citizen expect from such a morality-based society? The citizens of America present and future had (and have) a right to know what benefits they would obtain from an adherence to fundamental moral principles. The founders did not disappoint. They envisioned a more perfect union with freedom, liberty, justice, and equality for all Americans.

So equality is directly linked to our freedoms and to our system of liberty and justice for all. Giving someone a preference, lower academic requirements, contract set-asides, or employment quotas betrays that system. Preferences based on race and ethnicity diminish the value of the individual in ways too numerous to mention and have consequences far beyond their effects on the nation's character and the harm that they do to those who are not the beneficiaries of such policies. Preferences unwittingly damage the perceived beneficiaries more than one can ever imagine, despite the denials of preference advocates. This occurs in two principal ways.

> *"Preferences based on race and ethnicity diminish the value of the individual."*

First, preferential policies, by their nature, require a paradigm of victims and oppressors. In a highly competitive society such as America, nothing is more debilitating to an individual than to crush the competitive instinct. It is like taking a baby animal from its mother, domesticating it, and then turning it loose in the wilderness. The probability is high that the animal, its natural instincts to survive dulled by the process of domestication, will have a difficult time surviving in the wild. So it is with people, especially black people. Although their ancestors successfully struggled to overcome tremendous obstacles, many young blacks seem to be lacking in the area that matters most in a modern, global economy: a competitive desire and self-confidence in one's ability to compete in academic pursuits. Too many young, bright, black men and women have no confidence in themselves and in the American system when the subject is education.

The major obstacle facing the average black person in America is not race; it is the attitude and approach of black people toward their role in American society. If we have any hope of moving America forward in its attitudes toward race, we must get black people to acknowledge and act on their role in resolving this issue. This is not to suggest that black people alone can resolve the American race dilemma. Nor is it to suggest that white people have no obligation to come to terms with their role in resolving this dilemma. But too often the race dialogue centers on what "white America" must do and is totally neglectful of the role of black people.

The second effect is equally as consequential: preferences create their own "glass ceiling." I don't know why the defenders of such policies fail to acknowledge or admit the enormous effect that such policies have on the attitudes of others. Does it ever occur to them that the reason black people and other "minorities" are not considered for more upper management positions, even in corporations that pound their chests about "celebrating diversity," is that such corporations still consider "minorities" to be inferior and noncompetitive for higher positions? Giving people who are classified in a certain group a "leg up" stems from the view that those individuals have limited capacity and cannot succeed without someone else's generosity. Simply put, affirmative action marginalizes its beneficiaries.

The Challenge Ahead

The people of California and Washington have begun to grapple with and resolve issues of race and ethnicity. It is of vital importance that the people in the rest of the nation too begin to resolve these issues. Unless this national reform proceeds apace, a long period of quiet turmoil in America is likely to be the result. Ultimately, the turmoil may no longer be quiet.

Throughout the debate about race preferences, opponents as well as proponents summon the words of Dr. King to help make their case. Obviously, no one knows what position Dr. King would have taken on this issue if he were alive today. There is one statement that he made, however, that should go unchallenged, and it can serve us well in our time: "Sooner or later all the peoples of the world, without regard to the political systems under which they live, will have to discover a way to live together in peace."

As a nation, America has got itself into one hell of a mess because of affirmative action preferences. Some groups of people believe it is their entitlement while others are seething with anger about such programs. If the words of Dr. King are to come true, we must end the existing system of preferences that differentiates the American people on the basis of race, ethnicity, and gender. Only by doing that can we rededicate our nation to the principle of equality and bring social peace and harmony to America.

Affirmative Action Ignores Genuine Diversity

by Nat Hentoff

About the author: *Author and syndicated columnist Nat Hentoff writes for the* Village Voice *and for* Editor & Publisher.

As the term affirmative action came under increasing fire, its proponents in college admissions offices decided that diversity would be a far more appealing justification for racial preferences. As William Bowen of Princeton University enthused; "Students of different races, religions and backgrounds . . . learn from their differences and stimulate one another to reexamine even their most deeply held assumptions."

But when colleges got down to defining diversity, that seemingly expansive term often came up quite short.

Take the University of Washington Law School in Seattle. For years, it was in the forefront of giving preference to "underrepresented students." In 1996—as the law school admitted in a report to the American Bar Association and the American Association of Law Schools—it denied admittance to "a white welfare mother with good but not outstanding credentials" because the admissions committee decided that she was not someone who would contribute "significantly" to the diversity of the class, not being "a member of a racial or ethnic group subject to discrimination."

The white welfare mother was admitted to Harvard Law School. The admissions committee there grasped that, despite her lack of minority racial status, she might well contribute a diversity of experience to her classmates, not many of whom had ever been on welfare.

Granted, she seems to have come out ahead. Hopefully the onetime welfare mom is now a Harvard Law grad. But the problems of diversity aren't as easily solved. There is some good evidence that diversity in practice doesn't look anything like diversity in theory. And some even better evidence that achieving di-

Nat Hentoff, "All Mixed Up," *New Jersey Law Journal*, vol. 165, August 20, 2001, p. 19. Copyright © 2001 by American Lawyer Media Properties, Inc. Reproduced by permission.

versity through racial preferences is on a collision course with the dissonances of American life.

"I Really Resented It"

From the reporting I've seen—and done—on campuses where greater use of racial preferences is made, there is considerable evidence that the resultant diversity often leads to more isolation and misunderstanding.

In May 1999, Vinnee Tong, a student at the University of California-Berkeley, told the *New York Times:* "[W]hen you first get here . . . they give you this talk about diversity, what kind of place did you come from, what kind of people did you live with? They really shove that down your throat. I come from a predominantly white, Republican town in Northern California, and all of a sudden I'm an Asian girl, whether I like it or not. I really resented it."

Such diversity doesn't seem to lead to closer relations in the way its proponents hoped. The *Chronicle of Higher Education*, looking at affirmative action at the University of Michigan in October 1998, noted that students' close friendships tended to be with people of their own race. When I taught at Princeton University a few years ago, I was given a similar picture by both black and white students.

Some mutual illumination between students with different life stories does happen, of course. But on many campuses, I've heard from white students who wanted to talk but were rebuffed by black students who preferred to be among themselves. It seems that setting some individuals up as objects of diversity for the benefit of others doesn't actually close the divide between them.

In their book, *When Hope and Fear Collide: A Portrait of Today's College Students*, Arthur Levine, president of Teachers College, Columbia University, and Jeanette Cureton, an educational researcher, reported that "students were most troubled about race relations on those campuses in which diverse groups had the greatest opportunity for sustained contact."

Levine explained in the *New York Times* in June 2000: "[D]iversity is the largest cause of student unrest on campus, accounting for 39 percent of student protests, according to our study. Discourse is dominated by two small, but vociferous groups—one yelling that diversity has eclipsed all other aspects of college life, and the other shouting that colleges remain impervious to diversity. Meanwhile, the rest of the campus community tries to avoid the issue."

> *"So is a student more 'diverse' if she has one white parent and one Latino parent, or less 'diverse'? . . . In awarding preferences, which drop of blood counts?"*

Consider this illustration of diversity in full exclusionary flower. UCLA's [University of California, Los Angeles] student newspaper, the *Daily Bruin*, [in 2000] listed a multiplicity of graduation ceremonies, in addition to the "traditional" ceremony. Such separate rites, supposedly dedicated to "making student groups comfortable," included the Samahang Philipino Celebration; the Iranian Student Group Ceremony; the Lavender Ceremony for lesbian, gay, bisexual, and transgender students; and the African-American Student Union Graduation Ceremony.

In short, diversity seems to be further dividing at least as many people as it's bringing together.

Tailoring Diversity

There is another dimension of diversity that will present extraordinary, and maybe insuperable, challenges to college admissions, even if the Supreme Court decides that current race-preference policies are constitutional if they are narrowly tailored (which is debatable).

John Skrentry, associate professor of sociology at the University of California-San Diego, explores problems of defining diversity that will render any decision the Supreme Court makes inconclusive and ultimately irrelevant. Many colleges now include Latinos and Native Americans among those accorded preferences. But Skrentry pointed out in the Feb. 16, [2001], *Chronicle of Higher Education*, they apparently "make no distinction between Latino students born in the United States and those born in Spain, Latin America, or other countries—nor [between] black students born here and those who are immigrants, or the children of immigrants, from the West Indies or Africa."

> *"We undermine the strength of our growing diversity when we chain its recognition to allegedly distinct racial and ethnic categories."*

At the University of Michigan undergraduate schools, and at other colleges where additional points are added to the admissions scores of Latinos, Skrentry asked "whether someone who is half or quarter-Latino should get all [the points], or whether Mexican or Puerto Rican applicants deserve more points than Salvadoran or Cuban applicants, or whether a recent Latino immigrant should receive all the points, and so on."

How will the NAACP [National Association for the Advancement of Colored People] Legal Defense Fund, the American Civil Liberties Union, the Congressional Black Caucus and other paladins of affirmative action, wondered Skrentry, regard preferences being given to "people with no historical experience of severe discrimination anything close to what black people have experienced in this country"?

In short, how can college admissions committees searching for diversity or courts looking for discrimination sort out individuals from all these underrepresented groups—including individuals who have not personally suffered any discrimination at all?

Chapter 3

Census 2000

Even more difficult to parse is the implication of Census 2000 for diversity standards. As reported in the April 8, [2001], *New York Times:* "Children under the age of 18 . . . are twice as likely [as adults] to identify themselves as being of more than one race." In total, 6.8 million Americans told the Census Bureau that they are members of two or more races. To further complicate the problem, 80 percent of those who identified themselves as biracial listed white as one of those races.

The May 15, [2001], *Race Relations Reporter*, also citing Census 2000, noted: "There are now 1.5 million mixed-race marriages, a tenfold increase since 1960. . . . Asians and Hispanics are the most likely ethnic groups to marry a person from another group."

So is a student more "diverse" if she has one white parent and one Latino parent, or less "diverse"? What if she has three white grandparents and one Asian grandparent? In awarding preferences, which drop of blood counts?

All of which begs the question: What about the very concept of race itself? Won't the courts, at some point, have to address the issue of what race is?

In *The Emperor's New Clothes: Biological Theories of Race at the Millennium*, Joseph Graves Jr., professor of evolutionary biology at Arizona State University West, argued that the very concept of race is "demonstrably false." He pointed out in the April 6, [2001], *Chronicle of Higher Education*: "There are not enough genetic differences between disparate groups of humans, and no human populations have unique evolutionary lineages. They've all had enough gene flow so that they can't be considered distinct."

Diversity in America, among Americans, is undeniably a good thing. Indeed, it's one of our greatest strengths. But although many Americans still think—and some discriminate—in terms of race, we undermine the strength of our growing diversity when we chain its recognition to allegedly distinct racial and ethnic categories.

As University of Michigan Law Professor Deborah Malamud wrote in her essay in the book *Color Lines:* "We should recognize that legalization of the forms of color-consciousness we endorse also makes it difficult to abolish the forms of color-consciousness we abhor." Preferences in college admissions ought to be based on real differences among individuals, not categories.

Affirmative Action Fosters Equal Opportunity

by Wilbert Jenkins

About the author: *Wilbert Jenkins is a history professor at Temple University in Philadelphia, Pennsylvania.*

The historical origins of affirmative action can be found in the 14th and 15th Amendments to the Constitution, the Enforcement Acts of 1870 and 1871, and the Civil Rights Acts of 1866 and 1875, which were passed by Republican-dominated Congresses during the Reconstruction period. This legislation set the precedent for many of the civil rights laws of the 1950s and 1960s—such as the Civil Rights Act of 1957, the Civil Rights Act of 1964, and the Voting Rights Act of 1965—and paved the way for what would become known as affirmative action.

In spite of the fact that laws designed to promote and protect the civil and political rights of African-Americans were enacted by Congress in the 1950s and 1960s, it was obvious that racism and discrimination against blacks in the area of education and, by extension, the workplace were huge obstacles that needed to be overcome if African-Americans were ever going to be able to carve an economic foundation. Thus, in the 1960s, affirmative action became a part of a larger design by President Lyndon Johnson's War on Poverty program. In a historic 1965 speech at Howard University, the nation's top black school, Johnson illustrated the thinking that led to affirmative action: "You do not take a person who for years has been hobbled by chains and liberate him, bring him to the starting line and say you are free to compete with all the others." Civil rights leader Martin Luther King, Jr., also underscored this belief when he stated that "one cannot ask people who don't have boots to pull themselves up by their own bootstraps."

A Fighting Chance

Policymakers fervently believed that more than three centuries of enslavement, oppression, and discrimination had so economically deprived African-

Americans that some mechanism had to be put in place that would at least allow them a fighting chance. Blacks were locked out of the highest paid positions and made considerably fewer dollars than their white counterparts in the same jobs. Moreover, the number of African-Americans enrolling in the nation's undergraduate and graduate schools was extremely low. Affirmative action became a vehicle to correct this injustice. The original intent of affirmative action was not to provide jobs and other advantages to blacks solely because of the color of their skin, but to provide economic opportunities for those who are competent and

> *"There is little evidence that those who have been aided by affirmative action policies feel many doubts or misgivings."*

qualified. Due to a history of discrimination, even those with outstanding credentials were often locked out. As the years wore on, it was deemed necessary to add other minorities—such as Native Americans, Hispanics, and Asian-Americans—as well as women to the list of those requiring affirmative action in order to achieve a measure of economic justice.

A number of conservatives—black and white—such as Armstrong Williams, Linda Chavez, Patrick Buchanan, Robert Novak, Ward Connerly, Clarence Thomas, Clint Bolick, Alan Keyes, and others argue that it is time to scrap affirmative action. This is necessary, they maintain, if the country is truly going to become a color-blind society like King envisioned. People would be judged by the content of their character, not by the color of their skin. Many among these conservatives also maintain that affirmative action is destructive to minorities because it is demeaning, saps drive, and leads to the development of a welfare dependency mentality. Minorities often come to believe that something is owed them.

Thus, conservatives argue against race-based admissions requirements to undergraduate and graduate schools, labeling them preferential treatment and an insult to anyone who is the beneficiary of this practice. In their opinion, it is psychologically, emotionally, and personally degrading for individuals to have to go through life realizing they were not admitted to school or given employment because of their credentials, but in order to fill some quota or to satisfy appearances. It is rather ironic, however, that they are so concerned about this apparent harm to black self-esteem, since there is little evidence that those who have been aided by affirmative action policies feel many doubts or misgivings. The vast majority of them believe they are entitled to whatever opportunities they have received—opportunities, in their estimation, which are long overdue because of racism and discrimination. Consequently, America is only providing them with a few economic crumbs which are rightfully theirs.

What the Facts Reveal

Although a number of affirmative action critics argue that lowering admissions standards for minorities creates a class of incompetent professionals—if they are somehow fortunate enough to graduate—the facts run counter to their arguments. For instance, a study conducted by Robert C. Davidson and Ernest L. Lewis of affirmative action students admitted to the University of California Medical School with low grades and test scores concluded that these students became doctors just as qualified as the higher-scoring applicants. The graduation rate of 94% for special-admissions students compared favorably to that of regular-admissions students (98%). Moreover, despite the fact that regular-admissions students were more likely to receive honors or A grades, there was no difference in the rates at which students failed core courses.

Many whites have been the recipients of some form of preferential treatment. For many years, so-called selective colleges have set less-demanding standards for admitting offspring of alumni or the children of the rich and famous. For example, though former Vice President Dan Quayle's grade-point average was minuscule and his score on the LSAT [Law School Admission Test] very low, he was admitted to Indiana University's Law School. There is little evidence that Quayle or other re-

> *"Affirmative action has produced some tangible benefits for the nation as a whole."*

cipients of this practice have developed low self-esteem or have felt any remorse for those whose credentials were better, but nonetheless were rejected because less-qualified others took their slots. The following example further underscores this practice. A number of opponents of affirmative action were embarrassed during 1996 in the midst of passage of Proposition 209, which eliminated affirmative action in California, when the *Los Angeles Times* broke a story documenting the fact that many of them and their children had received preferential treatment in acquiring certain jobs and gaining entry to some colleges.

Some opponents of affirmative action go so far as to suggest that it aggravates racial tensions and leads, in essence, to an increase in violence between whites and people of color. This simply does not mesh with historical reality. Discrimination against and violence toward the powerless always [have] increased during periods of economic downturns, as witnessed by the depressions of 1873 and 1893. There was nothing akin to affirmative action in this country for nearly two centuries of its existence, yet African-American women were physically and sexually assaulted by whites, and people of color were brutalized, murdered, and lynched on an unprecedented scale. Moreover, there were so many race riots in the summer of 1919 that the author of the black national anthem, James Weldon Johnson, referred to it as "the red summer." The 1920s witnessed the reemergence of a reinvigorated Ku Klux Klan. Many state politicians even went public with their memberships, and the governor of Indiana during this period was an avowed member of the Klan. The 1930s and 1940s did not bring much relief, as attested to by several race riots and President Franklin D. Roosevelt's refusal to promote an antilynching bill.

Some of the African-American critics of affirmative action have actually been beneficiaries of such a program. It is unlikely that Clarence Thomas would have been able to attend Yale University Law School or become a justice on the U.S. Supreme Court without affirmative action. Yet, Thomas hates it with a passion, once saying he would be violating "God's law" if he ever signed his name to an opinion that approved the use of race—even for benign reasons—in hiring or admissions.

No Proof of Reverse Discrimination

Opponents of affirmative action from various racial and ethnic backgrounds argue that it may lead to reverse discrimination, whereby qualified whites fail to acquire admission to school, secure employment, or are fired because of their race since prospective slots have to be preserved solely for minorities. It is difficult to say with any degree of certainty how many whites may have been by-passed or displaced because preferences have been given to blacks and other minorities. What can be said, though, with a large measure of accuracy is that whites have not lost ground in medicine and college teaching, despite considerable efforts to open up those fields. In addition, contrary to popular myth, there is little need for talented and successful advertising executives, lawyers, physicians, engineers, accountants, colleges professors, movie executives, chemists, physicists, airline pilots, architects, etc. to fear minority preference. Whites who lose out are more generally blue-collar workers or persons at lower administrative levels, whose skills are not greatly in demand.

Furthermore, some whites who are passed over for promotion under these circumstances may simply not be viewed as the best person available for the job. It is human nature that those not receiving promotions that go to minorities or not gaining admission to colleges and universities prefer to believe that they have been discriminated against. They refuse to consider the possibility that the minorities could be better qualified. Although some highly qualified white students may be rejected by the University of California

> *"It is of paramount importance that as many educational opportunities as possible be extended to the nation's minorities."*

at Berkeley, Duke, Yale, Harvard, Stanford, or Princeton, the same students often are offered slots at Brown, Dartmouth, Cornell, Columbia, Michigan, the University of Pennsylvania, and the University of North Carolina at Chapel Hill—all first-rate institutions of higher learning. . . .

Tangible Benefits

Affirmative action has produced some tangible benefits for the nation as a whole. As a result of it, the number of minorities attending and receiving degrees from colleges and universities rose in the 1970s and 1980s. This led to an increase in the size of the African-American middle class. An attainment of higher levels of education, as well as affirmative action policies in hiring, helped blacks gain access to some professions that earlier had been virtually closed to them. For instance, it traditionally had been nearly impossible for African-Americans and other minorities to receive professorships at predominantly white schools. Some departments at these schools actively began to recruit and hire minority faculty as their campuses became more diverse.

As expected, African-American, Hispanic, Native American, and Asian-American students demanded that not only should more minority faculty be hired, but that the curriculum be expanded to include courses that deal with the cultural and historical experiences of their past. Some school administrators granted their demands, which has borne fruit in a number of ways. First, given the fact that the U.S. is steadily becoming even more multicultural, it is imperative that Americans learn about and develop an appreciation and respect for various cultures. This could enable those who plan to teach students from several different racial, cultural, and ethnic backgrounds in the public school system to approach their jobs with more sensitivity and understanding. Second, it is often crucial for minority faculty to act as role models, particularly on white campuses. Third, white students could profit by being taught by professors of color. Since a white skin provides everyday advantages, having to face people of color in positions of authority may awaken some whites to realities about themselves and their society they previously have failed to recognize. It also might become obvious to them that certain racial stereotypes fly out of the window in light of intellectual exchanges with professors and peers of color.

> *"Now is the perfect time to find ways of improving affirmative action, rather than developing strategies aimed at destroying it."*

Since education is crucial to acquiring economic advancement, it is of paramount importance that as many educational opportunities as possible be extended to the nation's minorities, which many studies indicate will total 50% of the population by 2050. Although much more is needed than affirmative action in order for minorities to gain the necessary access to higher levels of education and hiring, it nevertheless is the best mechanism to ensure at least a small measure of success in this regard. However, it currently is under attack in the areas of higher education, hiring, and federal contracts. Now is the perfect time to find ways of improving affirmative action, rather than developing strategies aimed at destroying it. . . .

A Diverse Workforce Is a Plus

Many industries began downsizing in the late 1980s and the practice has continued in the 1990s, helping to reverse some of the earlier gains made by minorities. With American society steadily becoming even more multicultural, it makes good business sense to have a workforce that is reflective of this development. In order to make this a reality, affirmative action policies need to be kept in place, not abandoned. Why not use the expertise of African-Americans to target African-American audiences for business purposes or Asian-Americans to tap into potential Asian-American consumers? Businessmen who believe minorities will purchase products as readily from all-white companies as those which are perceived as diverse are seriously misguided.

> *"[People of color] merely are asking that some mechanism be kept in place to help provide the same social and economic opportunities most whites have had."*

A diverse workforce also can yield huge economic dividends in the international business sector, as became obvious in 1996 to Republicans who hoped to increase their majority in Congress and ride into the White House by attacking affirmative action policies in hiring. Representative Dan Burton of Indiana, Speaker of the House Newt Gingrich, and presidential candidate Bob Dole, to name a few, applied pressure on businesses to end affirmative action policies in hiring. Executives informed them that this would be bad business and that the losses in revenue potentially would be staggering. In addition, it would be foolish public relations and substantially would reduce the pool of fine applicants. For the time being, the Republicans eased off.

A diverse workforce in a multicultural society makes practical and ethical sense. With all of the problems that need to be solved—such as disease, hunger, poverty, homelessness, lack of health care, racism, anti-Semitism, sexism, teenage pregnancy, crime, drugs, etc.—why should anyone's input be limited because of sex, race, color, class, or ethnic background? All Americans should be working together in this endeavor. It can best be accomplished by creating a truly diverse workforce through a continuation of affirmative action policies.

An Ongoing Need

In spite of the fact that affirmative action has helped some African-Americans and other minorities achieve a middle-class status, not all have witnessed a significant improvement in their economic condition. For the most part, it has only helped the last generation of minorities. In order to make a significant impact, affirmative action policies need to be in place for several generations. Between 1970 and 1992, the median income for white families, computed in constant dollars, rose from $34,773 to $38,909, an increase of 11.9%. Black family income declined during this period, from $21,330 to $21,162. In relative terms, black incomes dropped from $613 to $544 for each $1,000 received by whites. Moreover, in 1992, black men with bachelor's degrees made $764 for each $1,000 received by white men with such degrees, and black males with master's degrees earned $870 for each $1,000 their white counterparts earned. Overall, black men received $721 for every $1,000 earned by white men.

Even more depressing for blacks is the fact that unemployment rates for them have remained at double-digit levels since 1975, averaging 14.9% for the 1980s, while the average was 6.3% for whites. The number of black children living below the poverty line reached 46.3% by 1992, compared to 12.3% of white children. At the same time, the overall poverty rate among Hispanics increased to 28.2%. Even in professions where blacks made breakthroughs by the early 1990s, they remained underrepresented. This was the case in engineering, law, medicine, dentistry, architecture, and higher education. Although blacks represented 10.2% of the workforce in 1992, they constituted just 3.7% of engineers, 2.7% of dentists, 3.1% of architects, and held 4.8% of university faculty positions.

Furthermore, while 27,713 doctoral degrees were awarded in 1992 to U.S. citizens and aliens who indicated their intention to remain in America, 1,081, or 3.9%, of these doctorates went to blacks. Given the low percentage of African-Americans receiving doctoral degrees, most college departments in all likelihood will find it difficult to recruit black faculty. With the hatchet steadily chopping affirmative action programs, this may become virtually impossible in the near future. The same holds true for other professions.

The most feasible way to ensure that colleges, universities, and various occupations will not become lily-white again is by the continuation of affirmative action. It gives minority groups that traditionally have been locked out of the education system and the workforce the best opportunity to carve out a solid economic foundation in America. I agree with President [Bill] Clinton, who said, "Don't end it, mend it."

America has had over 200 years to deliver true justice, freedom, and equality to women and people of color. To believe that it now will make good the promise of equality without some kind of legislation to assist it is to engage in fantasy.

In advocating for affirmative action policies, people of color are not looking for government handouts. They merely are asking that some mechanism be kept in place to help provide the same social and economic opportunities most whites have had and continue to have access to.

Affirmative Action Should Not Be Eliminated

by Harry P. Pachon

About the author: *Harry P. Pachon is president of the Tomas Rivera Policy Institute and a professor of public policy at Claremont Graduate University in Claremont, California.*

A good way to measure the impact of Proposition 209, the initiative that widely eliminated affirmative action in California, is to analyze the regulations the University of California (UC) adopted to mirror the proposition. The UC trustees rescinded these regulations in late May [2001]. Therefore, a look at the data from 1998 to 2000, when these regulations were in force, shows the effect of eliminating racial and ethnic preferences in college admissions and may be illustrative of the overall impact of the Proposition 209 initiative.

Across all eight UC campuses, admission rates for black and Latino students dropped by more than 25 percent. At the flagship campuses—Berkeley and UCLA (University of California at Los Angeles)—the drop was even more dramatic. Blacks experienced more than a 50 percent drop in admissions, and Latino rates fell more than 40 percent. As a result, there were 2,100 fewer black and Latino freshmen in the class of 2001 than in the class of 1997 at Berkeley and UCLA. Systemwide, this number was 6,500. These drops occurred while the proportion of black and Latino high-school graduates in the applicant pool increased. For example, Latino applications to all UC campuses increased by two-thirds [between 1998 and 2001].

The Reality of University Admissions

If UC rejected a higher number of minorities, Proposition 209 supporters argue that California is better off in the long run because a meritocracy has been re-established in the state's top public universities. But a look at the reality of the UC admissions process belies the assumptions of those arguing that affirmative action subverts meritocracy.

Some, but not all California public high-school students can take advanced placement (AP) courses, which give them two advantages: (1) They increase their grade-point averages because a grade in an AP course counts one point higher than a regular course grade, and (2) they test out of selected college courses if they pass an AP examination. Therefore, it is possible for students to graduate with a grade-point average above 4.0 and to have met some of their undergraduate course requirements. It also is not unusual for universities such as Berkeley and UCLA to turn down students who have averages higher than 4.0.

> *"Affirmative action was a method college-admissions officers used to get around the educational inequalities built into the state's public high schools."*

Why is this relevant to the affirmative-action debate and the impact of Proposition 209? A closer look at AP courses in California public high schools, as revealed by a Tomas Rivera Policy Institute study, highlights that while some high schools offer as many as 30 AP courses, other high schools offer only one or two of these classes. Some don't offer any AP courses. Moreover, high schools with larger proportions of minority students are less likely to offer AP courses.

Therefore, when making admissions decisions, universities place students from predominantly minority schools at an automatic disadvantage because they have neither the higher grade-point averages nor the opportunity to take courses that present the intellectual challenges of AP courses. While educational inequalities in AP courses continue to exist, UC campuses listed the "number of AP courses taken" as part of their admissions criteria until several years ago.

AP courses provide only one example of how existing educational inequities compromise merit. A similar review of college-admissions tests would reveal that "merit" also is tainted because economically privileged students can take preparatory courses to improve their SATs.

Whatever its deficiencies, affirmative action was a method college-admissions officers used to get around the educational inequalities built into the state's public high schools. With the elimination of affirmative action through Proposition 209 the identification of and outreach to meritorious minority students was dealt a serious setback.

Five Meanings of Affirmative Action

My identification of affirmative action with merit may be puzzling to some. The reason for this is simple. The Proposition 209 debate defined affirmative action as being linked with racial and ethnic preferences. However, there are at least five different meanings for affirmative action. To understand the affirmative-action debate, it's important to understand all these meanings:

• First, affirmative action simply may mean that an employer or institution will follow nondiscrimination in regard to gender or racial bias.

• Second, it may mean affirmative recruitment, in which an employer or organization makes special efforts to recruit and reach out to women and minorities.

• Third, affirmative action also may mean affirmative fairness, in which the special circumstances of individuals are taken into account when they are considered for jobs or admissions.

• Fourth, it also can be affirmative preference, in which, with all things being equal, preference is given to individuals from such underrepresented groups as women and minorities.

• Fifth, and finally, affirmative action also can stand for quotas, in which individuals who meet minimum requirements are selected over more-qualified applicants to meet numerical goals established by an institution or by government.

Anecdotes Do Not Reveal the Truth

The fourth and, especially, fifth definitions of affirmative action are the ones critics use to set up an easily identifiable target. Yet to what extent is affirmative action, as currently practiced by American corporations, educational institutions and the government, really affirmative fairness or affirmative recruitment?

The answer is that we simply don't know. And because we don't know, the anecdote rules the day. We hear stories of poor white students denied admission into colleges because wealthy children of wealthy black physicians receive "preference." Are these stories representative of reality?

> *"Affirmative action . . . overcomes some of the institutional biases and discriminatory practices still plaguing American society."*

If we follow the critics' logic, American institutions should be awash with women and minorities displacing victimized white males, while minorities receive the largest share of government contracts. Yet when supporters of affirmative action attempt to use data to show that this is not the case, their claims are dismissed. For example, when you compare the salaries of 25- to 29-year-old African-American, Latino and women managers in the California private sector to their white male counterparts, the salary differential ranges from $3,500 to $8,700.

In California, for every Mexican-American male manager in private industry, there are 20 white male managers. When statistics such as these are presented, they are dismissed by critics of affirmative action as being somewhat illegitimate. Yet how do they buttress their points attacking affirmative action? They refer to statistics! Phrases such as "Seventy percent of all African-Americans drop out of college" are used. Evidently, in the current affirmative-action debate, a double standard exists. Statistics that demonstrate racial and gentler underrepresentation are not valid. Statistics that show failure on the part of affirmative action, however, are kosher.

Since data from either side will not settle the current debate on the positive or negative impacts of Proposition 209, let me attempt to recast it in ideological terms. Rather than viewing affirmative action as merit vs. entitlement or individualism vs. entitlement, we need to consider that affirmative action is a continuation of this country's commitment to rewarding merit—no matter what the sex or ethnic background of the individual.

Affirmative Fairness

Affirmative action, defined as affirmative fairness and affirmative recruitment, seeks out talented and qualified individuals among the nation's 50 million people of African-American or Latino heritage. Consider the following: Do any of us really think the qualities of intelligence are genetically different among black, Latino or Anglo infants at birth? Aren't there outside variables that account for the fact that, after 20 years, these same African-American and Latino infants are young adults with test scores and grade-point averages lower than their white counterparts? Do substandard schools and unequal employment opportunities have any role in these differences?

Affirmative action, defined as affirmative recruitment and affirmative fairness, overcomes some of the institutional biases and discriminatory practices still plaguing American society. There is a wealth of talent in the barrios and ghettos of this nation tragically going untapped.

Sure, before Proposition 209, affirmative action was not perfect. Yet what program is? Moreover, as our conservative friends tell us, "the perfect should not be the enemy of the good." Supporters of affirmative action, and those opposed to Proposition 209, however, are losing the battle of semantics. As long as they allow the debate to be framed in terms of merit vs. entitlement or unqualified preferences, they will lose.

Proposition 209, overwhelmingly passed by the California white majority electorate and overwhelmingly rejected by the state's black and Latino voters (three out of four of whom voted against the initiative), is a draconian solution. It equates affirmative action with simple and semantically loaded words such as "quotas" and "preferences." It disregards the potential of linking affirmative action with the identification of merit.

Secretary of State Colin Powell, former chairman of the Joint Chiefs of Staff, links affirmative action with merit when he says, "I benefited from affirmative action in the Army, not because I was a quota promotion or someone said, 'He's black, move him ahead.' I benefited from affirmative action in the Army because the Army said, 'We're all going to be equal.'"

Proposition 209, as a public policy, may be a case of throwing the baby out with the bathwater. It has not allowed a nuanced discussion of how we can overcome educational and other inequalities that are correlated with racial and ethnic status.

It is not a level playing field. It is not a colorblind society.

Chapter 4

How Can Racial Problems Be Resolved?

Chapter Preface

In the late 1990s the Clinton administration convened a multiracial advisory panel to launch a national "initiative on race"—an ambitious project entailing research on racial issues, dozens of community dialogues on race relations, and proposals for resolving racial problems. In its 1998 report, *One America in the Twenty-First Century: Forging a New Future*, the advisory board presents several suggestions for improving race relations, including the recommendation that educators teach in a way that "accurately reflects our history from the perspective of all Americans, not just the majority population." The report goes on to assert that "teaching a more inclusive and comprehensive history is just one of the ways we may begin to become more comfortable about our nation's growing diversity."

Part of the incentive for starting this initiative on race, the panel maintains, was to confront Americans' concerns over their nation's anticipated demographic changes. Research suggests that by the year 2050 the U.S. Asian, Hispanic, black, and mixed-race population will increase significantly, while the white population will decrease from a current 74 percent to about 53 percent of the total population. Many analysts believe that if the United States is to persevere as the world's first truly multiracial democracy, Americans must fully welcome the country's increasing diversity and build communities based on shared values and respect for differences. The advisory panel on race suggests several concrete actions that individuals could take to help resolve racial problems. These suggestions include: consistently observe how issues of racial prejudice and privilege affect all people; make a conscious effort to get to know those of other races; initiate constructive dialogues on race in workplaces and schools; support institutions that promote racial inclusion; and participate in community projects to reduce racial disparities in opportunity.

Not everyone agrees that embracing racial diversity is a good idea. According to Michael S. Berliner and Gary Hull, analysts for the Ayn Rand Institute in Marina Del Rey, California, "'ethnic diversity' is merely racism in a politically correct disguise." In their opinion, the "diversity movement" actually fosters racism by encouraging the belief that one's character, identity, and culture are determined by skin color, eye shape, or other physical traits. While diversity proponents may espouse tolerance, they are doomed to fail because, as Berliner and Hull maintain, "One cannot teach students that their identity is determined by skin color and expect them to become colorblind. One cannot espouse multiculturalism and expect students to see each other as individual human beings." They believe that a better way to eradicate racism is to promote a "diversity of ideas" and to judge people by their individual characteristics.

Social analysts may disagree about the value of racial diversity, but America's dialogue on race relations is ongoing. As the following chapter shows, debates about reparations for slavery, racial profiling, and examinations of white privilege continue to capture the public's attention. One may be tempted to conclude that such stark differences of opinion on race relations is reason for pessimism about the future of a multiracial America. Yet many concerned observers, such as Harvard law professor Randall Kennedy, maintain that Americans should approach racial issues with a sense of hope. In Kennedy's opinion, such optimism "acknowledges our massive problems but also recognizes that, through intelligent collective action, we can meet and overcome them. . . . We can realistically expect to build on past accomplishments and press further."

Blacks Should Be Given Reparations for Slavery

by Manning Marable

About the author: *Manning Marable directs African American Studies at Columbia University and writes a weekly newspaper column distributed nationwide.*

The question of reparations for slavery is more than an intellectual exercise. In 1854, my great-grandfather was auctioned off for $500. The sale was "business as usual" for his white slave master in Georgia; for my family and for countless other African Americans, it was an affront against our humanity.

What I call the First Reconstruction (1865–1877) ended almost 250 years of legal slavery. But the four million people of African descent in this country anticipated not just personal freedom but also economic self-sufficiency. Thus African Americans clamored for "forty acres and a mule" as part of their compensation for more than two centuries of unpaid labor.

But compensation ("reparations") never came during this First Reconstruction. And with the rise of Jim Crow and legalized segregation, African Americans were firmly relegated to secondary status.

What I call the Second Reconstruction (1954–1968), or the modern Civil Rights Movement, outlawed legal segregation in public accommodations and gave Blacks voting rights. Yet the damaging legacy of slavery and of a century of legal segregation was never addressed.

Because neither the First nor the Second Reconstruction resolved the issue of compensation, this society has never truly confronted the reality that the disproportionate wealth that most whites enjoy today was first constructed from centuries of unpaid Black labor.

Not Just About Compensation

Demanding reparations is not just about compensation for the legacy of slavery and Jim Crow, however. Equally important, it is an education campaign that acknowledges the pattern of white privilege and Black inequality that is at the core of American history and that continues to this day.

White Americans today are not guilty of carrying out slavery and legal segregation. But whites have a moral and political responsibility to acknowledge the continuing burden of history's structural racism.

Structural racism's barriers include "equity-inequity," the absence of Black capital formation that is a direct consequence of America's history. One third of all Black households, for example, actually have negative net wealth. Black families are denied home loans at twice the rate of whites. Blacks remain the last hired and first fired during recessions. Blacks have significantly shorter life expectancies, in part due to racism in the health establishment. Blacks, by and large, attend inferior schools.

> *"The disproportionate wealth that most whites enjoy today was first constructed from centuries of unpaid Black labor."*

Reparations don't necessarily mean monetary payment to individuals. A reparations trust fund could be established, with the goal of closing the socioeconomic gaps between Blacks and whites. Funds would be targeted specifically toward poor, disadvantaged communities with the greatest need, not to individuals.

For decades, the call for Black reparations had been a central tenet in the political philosophy of Black Nationalist organizations and leaders, from Marcus Garvey to Elijah Muhammad. Beginning in the 1980s, support for reparations began to build. References to "forty acres and a mule" and reparations became popularized in hip-hop music and culture. [Film director] Spike Lee, for example, named his production company "40 acres and a mule" to make the political point that African Americans rarely owned the corporations that profited from black cultural production and commercialization. In April 2000, Chicago became the first major U.S. city to hold public hearings on the issue of the damaging legacy of slavery on African Americans. Congressman Bobby Rush spoke, declaring that "the future of race relations will be determined by reparations for slavery." Noted historian Lerone Bennett, author of *Before the Mayflower*, testified, "We're not talking about welfare. We're talking about back pay."

The Movement's Manifesto

In 2000, Randall Robinson, founder and president of Transafrica, published *The Debt: What America Owes to Blacks:* with the book, the modern reparations movement found its manifesto. *The Debt* warned that if "African Americans will not be compensated for the massive wrongs and social injuries inflicted upon them by their government during and after slavery, then there is no chance that America will solve its racial problems."

[In the spring of 2001], historian John Hope Franklin wrote an eloquent rebuttal to the argument of right-winger David Horowitz that the idea of reparations is racist. Dr. Franklin observed that all white Americans, even those who had not owned slaves, benefited materially and psychologically from "having a group beneath them. . . . Most living Americans do have a connection with slavery. They have inherited the preferential advantage, if they are white, or the loathsome disadvantage, if they are Black; and those positions are virtually as alive today as they were in the 19th century. The pattern of housing, the discrimination in employment, the resistance to equal opportunity in education, the racial profiling, the inequalities in the administration of justice, the low expectation of Blacks in the discharge of duties assigned to them, the widespread belief that Blacks have physical prowess but little intellectual capacities, and the widespread opposition to affirmative action, as if that had not been enjoyed by whites for three centuries—all indicate that the vestiges of slavery are still with us."

The racial dialogue in this country has, in recent decades, moved from "civil rights" to "multicultural diversity" and now to "reparations." In many ways, the first two categories are premised on the belief that racism is a consequence of ignorance or social isolation between groups. Reparations, however, takes a different vantage point: that racism is a logical and deliberate expression of the deep structures of white power and privilege in this country.

"Reparations" could begin America's Third Reconstruction, a chance to raise fundamental questions about the racialized character of power within our democracy. As scholar Robert Hill of UCLA [the University of California in Los Angeles] observed recently, the campaign for Black reparations is "the final chapter in the five hundred year struggle to suppress the transatlantic slave trade, slavery, and the consequences of its effects."

Blacks Should Not Be Given Reparations for Slavery

by John McWhorter

About the author: *John McWhorter teaches linguistics at the University of California in Berkeley.*

My childhood was a typical one for a black American in his mid-thirties. I grew up middle class in a quiet, safe neighborhood in Philadelphia [Pennsylvania]. I still miss living at the top of the tidy little cul-de-sac known as Marion Lane, and to this day there are few things more soothing to me than a walk through Carpenter's Woods across the street.

I didn't grow up in a segregated world. My parents didn't live "just enough for the city," as the old Stevie Wonder song goes; my mother taught social work at Temple University and my father was a student activities administrator there. My parents were far from wealthy, living at the edge of their credit cards like many middle class people. But I had everything I needed plus some extras, and spent more time in one of our two cars than on buses.

Contrary to popular belief, I was by no means extraordinarily "lucky" or "unusual" among black Americans of the post–Civil Rights era. There was a time when the childhood I've just described was the province of a tiny "black bourgeoisie." (In 1940, for example, only one in a hundred black families had a middle class income.) But today, there are legions of black adults in the United States who grew up as I did. As a child, I never had trouble finding black peers, and as an adult, meeting black people with life histories like mine requires no searching. In short, in our moment, black success is a norm. Less than one in four black families now live below the poverty line, and the black underclass is at most one out of five blacks. This is what the Civil Rights revolution helped make possible, and I grew up exhilarated at belonging to a race that had made such progress in the face of many obstacles.

John McWhorter, "Blood Money," *The American Enterprise*, vol. 12, July 2001, p. 18. Copyright © 2001 by *The American Enterprise*, a magazine of Politics, Business, and Culture. On the web at www.TAEmag. com. Reproduced by permission.

Yet today, numerous black officials tell the public that lives like mine are statistical noise, that the overriding situation for blacks is one of penury, dismissal, and spiritual desperation. Under this analysis, the blood of slavery remains on the hands of mainstream America until it allocates a large sum of money to "repair" the unsurmounted damage done to our race over four centuries.

The ideological impulses infecting black America since the mid-1960s make a "reparations" movement not just logical but almost predictable. Yet the notion is a distraction from the real work we have to do.

Reparations or Blood Money?

The shorthand version of the reparations idea is that living blacks are "owed" the money that our slave ancestors were denied for their unpaid servitude. But few black Americans even know the names or life stories of their slave ancestors; almost none of us have pictures or keepsakes from that far back. I am relatively unique even in happening to know my most recent slave ancestor's name—it was also John Hamilton McWhorter. Yes, my slave ancestors were "blood" to me; yes, what was done to them was unthinkable. But the 150 years between me and them has rendered our tie little more than biological. Paying anyone for the suffering of long-dead strangers, even if technically relatives, would be more a matter of blood money than "reparation."

Quite simply, for me to reap a windfall from the first John Hamilton McWhorter's suffering would be a trivialization of his existence. He spent a life in unpaid and permanent servitude; I get paid because every now and then I get trailed by a salesclerk? Or even stopped on a drug check by a policeman? That would dishonor my ancestors' suffering.

Perhaps recognizing this, the reparations movement is now drifting away from the "back salary" argument to justifications emphasizing the effects of slavery since Emancipation. It is said blacks deserve payment for residual echoes of their earlier disenfranchisement and segregation. This justification, however, is predicated upon the misconception that in 2001, most blacks are "struggling."

This view denies the stunning success that the race has achieved over the past 40 years. It persists because many Americans, black and white, have accepted the leftist notion which arose in the mid-1960s that blacks are primarily victims in this country, that racism and structural injustice hobble all but a few individual blacks. Based on emotion, victimologist thought ignores the facts of contemporary black success and progress, because they do not square with the "blame game."

"The notion [of reparations] is a distraction from the real work we have to do."

The depictions of modern black America by reparations advocates—like Randall Robinson, author of *The Debt: What America Owes to Blacks*, who sees nothing but tragedy, scorn, and neglect for blacks in America—often sound even bleaker than analyses by black intellectuals at the turn of the [twentieth] century, when most blacks were still mired in poverty in the South. [Writer] W.E.B. Du Bois noted back in 1912 that blacks "have in a generation changed from a slave to a free labor system, reestablished family life, accumulated $1,000,000,000 [in] property, including 20,000,000 acres of land, and reduced their illiteracy from 80 to 30 percent."

One would never hear a modern "civil rights leader" make such a statement today, because it highlights black success rather than failure. This is a serious mistake. No valid appeal for reparations can be based on an inaccurate stereotype that "black" means "poor"—especially when the very people calling for reparations are so quick to decry this stereotype as racist when whites appeal to it.

Reparations cannot logically rely on a depiction of black Americans as a race still reeling from the brutal experience of slavery and its aftereffects. The reality is that, by any estimation, in the year 2001 there are more middle class blacks than poor ones. The large majority of black Americans, while surely not immune to the slings and arrows of the eternal injustices of life on earth, are now leading dignified lives as new variations on what it means to be American.

An argument for reparations that acknowledged the success and basic strength of black America today would aim squarely at the quarter or so of all blacks who are struggling, especially those in the inner cities. Even here, however, we must be

> *"Based on emotion, victimologist thought ignores the facts of contemporary black success and progress."*

careful about what "reparations" would be intended to do. If all black Americans living below the poverty line were given a subsidy to move to the suburbs, free tuition for college, and/or a small business loan, all indications are that it would make no difference in the overall condition of most of their lives in the long run. As the pitfalls of Section 8 programs in various cities have shown, a house in the suburbs cannot undo deeply ingrained cultural patterns etched by racism of the past but today self-generating.

Money to attend college is of little use in a culture that has inherited from the Black Power movement a tendency to equate scholarly commitment (beyond black-related topics) with "acting white." This pulls down the performance of even many middle class black students. The less privileged ones too often just drop out entirely.

The person who obtains a small business loan on his own can't help but have a deeper commitment to its success than the person who is simply handed a check from on high with no questions asked. This has been painfully clear from the checkered and often corrupt record of minority businesses that owe their existence to contracts meted out according to racial preferences.

The reality is that the only way for any group of human beings to succeed is through individual initiative. This may not be fair for a group with a history of oppression, but history records no other pathway to the top. In the mid-1960s, America experimented with the idea, a reasonable guess on its face, that simply giving handouts to poor blacks would enable them to bypass the conventional route to self-realization. But today the data are in: a three-generations-deep welfare culture where work was an option rather than a given, where a passive and victimhood-based relationship to mainstream accomplishment was endemic. There is nothing

> *"Any effort to repair problems in black America must focus on helping people to help themselves."*

"black" about this, given that similar policies have left an equally bleak situation in Native American communities, as well as white ones in Appalachia.

A "reparations" movement predicated upon the fiction that more brute handouts will raise large numbers of black people out of poverty would actually work against true and lasting uplift, leaving life nasty, brutish, and short for millions of black people. As the old adage goes—one which many blacks would spontaneously applaud—"Give a man a fish and he'll eat for a day, teach a man to fish and he'll eat forever."

Any effort to repair problems in black America must focus on helping people to help themselves. Funds must be devoted to ushering welfare mothers into working for a living, so that their children do not grow up learning that employment is something "other people" do. Inner city communities should be helped to rebuild themselves, in part through making it easier for residents to buy their homes. Police forces ought to be trained to avoid brutality, which turns young blacks against the mainstream today, and to work with, rather than against, the communities they serve.

Finally, this country must support all possible efforts to liberate black children from the soul-extinguishing influence of ossified urban public schools, and to move them into experimental or all-minority schools where a culture of competition is fostered. This will help undo the sense that intellectual excellence is a "white" endeavor. Surely we must improve the public schools as well, including increasing the exposure of young black children to standardized tests. But we also must make sure another generation of black children are not lost during the years it will take for these schools to get their acts together.

Most readers will have noticed that all of the things I just described are in fact taking place. George W. Bush's Faith-Based and Community Initiatives effort is a long-overdue attempt to bring black churches into play in helping make inner-city neighborhoods stable communities. Meanwhile, community development corporations are slowly working quiet wonders in such neighborhoods by granting inner-city people loans with which to purchase real estate. The Community Reinvestment Act concurrently spurs banks to make small business loans to minorities.

Numerous cities are demonstrating that cooperation between police forces and minority communities can lead to massive drops in crime. And the Bush administration is pressing to move minority children into functioning schools, while advocating increased testing of all students (though the Democrats' coddling of teachers' unions in return for votes presents a mighty obstacle).

In other words, it could be argued that America is already in the business of "reparations" for blacks, teaching us to fish instead of just giving us a dinner wrapped in newspaper.

"Reparations" Have Already Been Given

Furthermore, there have already been what any outside observer would term "reparations" since the 1960s. When reparations fans grouse that "It's time America acknowledged slavery," one wonders just what they thought the "War on Poverty" was. In the 1930s, welfare policies were primarily intended for widows. In the mid-1960s, welfare programs were deliberately expanded for the "benefit" of black people.

Federal and state governments have since poured billions of dollars into welfare payments and the imposing bureaucracy that grew up along with them. This very bureaucracy has gone on to provide secure government jobs for several million blacks. The byzantine industry of urban social service agencies familiar to us today did not exist before the late 1960s.

None of this was specifically termed "reparations," but it certainly provided unearned cash for underclass blacks for decades, as well as secure jobs for a great many others. Today, welfare programs are thankfully being recast as temporary stopgaps, with welfare mothers being trained for work. The funds and efforts devoted to this laudable effort are again a concrete attempt to overcome structural poverty. A society with no commitment to addressing the injustices of the past wouldn't bother with any of this effort aimed at poor blacks.

> *"Most reparations advocates are seeking. . . a comprehensive mea culpa by white America of responsibility for everything that ails any blacks."*

Affirmative action policies were similarly developed to acknowledge earlier slights. Initially intended as a call to recruit qualified blacks for hiring or school admission, the policy quickly transmogrified into quota systems, with lesser qualified blacks all too often being given positions over better qualified whites. Even most blacks under about age 45 tend to tacitly think of affirmative action as a "reparation," although they would not put it in just that way.

Despite the Herculean efforts we have seen over the past few decades, the sentiment persists among certain blacks that America somehow "owes" us still. These reparations advocates are at heart motivated by a broken self-image, a deep-seated insecurity about being black. This renders cries of victimhood imperative, because they are internally soothing. Black success is "beside the point" until all whites avidly "like" us. This is what blinds reparations advocates to the fact that most whites—especially educated and influential ones—long ago heard the message. It was Peter Edelman who resigned from the Clinton administration's Department of Health and Human Services over the reform of the welfare laws, and white former university presidents William Bowen and Derek Bok who penned the most prominent book-length defense of affirmative action, *The Shape of the River.*

Because the reparations movement is ultimately based on an inferiority complex rather than empirical engagement, the only "reparations" acceptable to its advocates would have to be officially titled as such, granted by a white America explicitly designating itself as the agent of all black misery past and present.

The problem is that no aid package could possibly have any substantial or lasting effect on black America unless it is designed to elicit self-generated initiative. And such packages are already in operation, though not titled as "reparations." Teaching disadvantaged blacks how to fish is exactly what the reform of welfare, the Office of Faith-Based and Community Initiatives, the community development corporations, the Community Reinvestment Act, the school voucher movement, and even the gradual rollback of racial preferences are all designed to do. A package of new handouts and set-asides, tied in a ribbon as a sop to black leaders' addiction to the giveaways of condescending white leftists, would not only have no serious benefit, it would do outright harm.

There would be damage on both sides of the racial divide. As the magic transformations of the package inevitably failed to appear, the flop would be attributed to there not having been enough money granted. Next a new mantra would become established in the black community to cover the bitter disappointment: "They think they can treat us like animals for four hundred years and then just pay us off?" Meanwhile, non-blacks would begin to grouse "They got reparations—what are they still complaining about?" Whether these mutterings would be valid is beside the point, what matters is that they would arise and be passed on to a new generation, to further poison interracial relations in this country.

Ultimately, a race shows its worth not by how much charity it can extract from others, but in how well it can do in the absence of charity. Black America has elicited more charity from its former oppressors than any race in human history—justifiably in my view. However, this can only serve as a spark—the real work is now ours.

Reforms Versus Pity

The only reparations I could live with are the substantial ones already in effect, which show all signs of making a difference to the minority of blacks left behind during the explosion of the black middle class. There are certainly some additional steps that could be taken to improve the chances of the black underclass:

increased child-care centers to make it easier for inner-city mothers to work; better transportation from cities to suburbs to make it easier to get to places of employment; more research on and funding for drug rehabilitation. There would be no harm in labeling a package of policies of this sort "reparations."

But in the end, most reparations activists would see this as "not enough." The reforms I've described are designed for the mundane business of concrete and measurable uplift. What most reparations advocates are seeking, on the other hand, is an emotional balm: a comprehensive mea culpa by white America of responsibility for everything that ails any blacks.

This version of "civil rights," however, is a mere excrescence of our moment—a competition for eliciting pity, which pre-1960s civil rights leaders would barely recognize. And it will pass.

Racial Profiling Should Be Abolished

by Randall Kennedy

About the author: *Randall Kennedy is a professor at Harvard Law School and the author of* Race, Crime, and the Law.

Consider the following case study in the complex interaction of race and law enforcement. An officer from the Drug Enforcement Administration [DEA] stops and questions a young man who has just stepped off a flight to Kansas City from Los Angeles. The officer has focused on this man for several reasons. Intelligence reports indicate that black gangs in Los Angeles are flooding the Kansas City area with illegal drugs, and the man in question was on a flight originating in Los Angeles. Young, toughly dressed, and appearing very nervous, he paid for his ticket in cash, checked no luggage, brought two carry-on bags, and made a beeline for a taxi upon deplaning. Oh, and one other thing: the officer also took into account the fact that the young man was black. When asked to explain himself, the officer declares that he considered the individual's race, along with other factors, because doing so helps him efficiently allocate the limited time and other resources at his disposal.

How should we evaluate the officer's conduct? Should we applaud it? Permit it? Prohibit it? As you think through this example, be aware that it is not a hypothetical one. Encounters like this take place every day, all over the country, as police attempt to battle street crime, drug trafficking, and illegal immigration. And this particular case study happens to be the fact pattern presented in a federal lawsuit of the early '90s, *United States v. Weaver*, in which the U.S. Court of Appeals for the Eighth Circuit upheld the constitutionality of the officer's action.

"Large groups of our citizens," the court declared, "should not be regarded by law enforcement officers as presumptively criminal based upon their race." The court went on to say, however, that "facts are not to be ignored simply because they may be unpleasant." According to the court, the circumstances were such that it made sense for the officer to regard blackness, when considered in conjunction with the other factors, as a signal that could be legitimately relied upon in the decision to approach and ultimately detain the suspect. "We wish it were otherwise," the court maintained, "but we take the facts as they are presented to us, not as we would like them to be." Other courts have agreed with the Eighth Circuit that the Constitution does not prohibit police from routinely taking race into account when they decide whom to stop and question, as long as they do so for purposes of bona fide law enforcement (not racial harassment) and as long as race is one of several factors that they consider.

Common Sense

These judicial decisions have been welcome news to the many police officers and other law enforcement officials who consider the racial selectivity of the sort deployed by the DEA agent an essential weapon in the war on crime. Such defenders of what has come to be known as racial profiling maintain that, in areas where young African American males commit a disproportionate number of the street crimes, the cops are justified in scrutinizing that sector of the population more closely than others—just as they are generally justified in scrutinizing men more closely than women. As Bernard Parks, chief of the Los Angeles Police Department, explained to Jeffrey Goldberg of the *New York Times Magazine:* "We have an issue of violent crime against jewelry salespeople. . . . The predominant suspects are Colombians. We don't find Mexican-Americans, or blacks, or other immigrants. It's a collection of several hundred Colombians who commit this crime. If you see six in a car in front of the Jewelry Mart, and they're waiting and watching people with briefcases, should we play the percentages and follow them? It's common sense."

For cops like Parks, racial profiling is a sensible, statistically based tool that enables them to focus their energies efficiently for the purpose of providing protection against crime to law-abiding folk. To borrow a concept from economics, it lowers the cost of obtaining and processing information, which in turn lowers the overall cost of doing the business of policing.

Moreover, the very fact that a number of cops who support racial profiling are black, like Parks, buttresses their claims that the practice isn't motivated by bigotry. Indeed, these police officers note that racial profiling is race-neutral in that various forms of it can be applied to persons of all races, depending on the circumstances. In predominantly black neighborhoods and other places in which white people

> *"Mere reasonableness is an insufficient justification for officials to discriminate on racial grounds."*

stick out in a suspiciously anomalous fashion (as potential drug customers or racist hooligans, for example), whiteness can become part of a profile. In the southwestern United States, where Latinos often traffic in illegal immigrants, apparent Latin American ancestry can become part of a profile. In a Chinatown where Chinese gangs appear to dominate certain criminal rackets, apparent Chinese ancestry can become part of a profile. Racial profiling, then, according to many cops, is good police work: a race-neutral, empirically based, and, above all, effective tool in fighting crime.

But the defenders of racial profiling are wrong. This, in itself, is not a particularly original claim. Indeed, ever since the Black and Latino Caucus of the New Jersey State Legislature held sensational hearings [in 1999], complete with testimony from victims of the New Jersey State Police force's allegedly overly aggressive racial profiling, the air has been thick with public denunciations of the practice. In June [1999], at a forum organized by the Justice Department on racial problems in law enforcement, President [Bill] Clinton condemned racial profiling as a "morally indefensible, deeply corrosive practice.". . .

Unfortunately, though, many who condemn racial profiling do so without really thinking the issue through. One common complaint about racial profiling is that using race (say, blackness) as one of several factors in selecting targets of surveillance is fundamentally and necessarily racist. But racial selectivity of this sort can be defended on nonracist grounds and is, in fact, embraced by people who are by no means anti-black bigots and are not even cops. Even Jesse Jackson once revealed himself to be an amateur racial profiler. "There is nothing more painful to me at this stage in my life," he said in 1993, "than to walk down the street and hear footsteps and start to think about robbery and then look around and see somebody white and feel relieved." The reason Jackson felt relief was not that he dislikes black people. He felt relief because he estimated, probably correctly, that he stood a somewhat greater risk of being robbed by a black person than by a white person.

> *"Taking race into account at all means engaging in racial discrimination."*

A second standard criticism of racial profiling involves a blanket denial of the central empirical claim upon which the practice rests: that in certain jurisdictions individuals associated with particular racial groups commit a disproportionate number of the crimes. But there's no use pretending that blacks and whites commit crimes (or are victims of crime) in exact proportion to their respective shares of the population. Statistics abundantly confirm that African Americans—and particularly young black men—commit a dramatically disproportionate share of street crime in the United States. This is a sociological fact, not a figment of the media's (or the police's) racist imagination. In recent years, for example, victims of crime report blacks as the perpetrators in around 25 percent of the violent crimes suffered, although blacks constitute only about twelve percent of the nation's population.

So, if racial profiling isn't necessarily bigoted, and if the empirical claim upon which the practice rests is sound, why is it wrong?

The argument begins with an insistence upon the special significance of racial distinctions in American life and law. Racial distinctions are and should be different from other lines of social stratification. That is why, since the civil rights revolution of the 1960s, courts have typically ruled—pursuant to the Fourteenth Amendment's equal protection clause—that mere reasonableness is an insufficient justification for officials to discriminate on racial grounds. In such cases, courts have generally insisted on applying "strict scrutiny"—the most intense level of judicial review—to the gov-

> *"Racial profiling constantly adds to the sense of resentment felt by blacks of every social stratum toward the law enforcement establishment."*

ernment's actions. Under this tough standard, the use of race in governmental decisionmaking may be upheld only if it serves a compelling government objective and only if it is "narrowly tailored" to advance that objective. Strict scrutiny embodies the recognition, forged in the difficult crucible of American history, that the presence of a racial factor in governmental decisionmaking gives rise to the presumption that officials may be acting in violation of someone's civil rights.

A disturbing feature of the debate over racial profiling is that many people, including judges, are suggesting that decisions distinguishing between persons on a racial basis do not constitute unlawful racial discrimination when race is not the sole consideration prompting disparate treatment. The court that upheld the DEA agent's detainment of the young black man at the Kansas City airport declined to describe the agent's action as racially discriminatory and thus evaded the requirement of subjecting the government's action to strict scrutiny. More recently, as Goldberg showed in his *New York Times Magazine* article, New Jersey Governor Christine Todd Whitman has been willing to denounce as wrongful racial discrimination only racial profiling in which "race is the only factor." For Whitman, when race is just one of a number of factors, the profiling ceases to be "racial" and becomes instead a defensible technique in which a police officer merely uses "cumulative knowledge and training to identify certain indicators of possible criminal activity." This dilution of the meaning of discrimination is troubling not only because it permits racial profiling to continue without adequate scrutiny. Even worse, this confusion will likely seep into other areas of racial controversy, causing mischief along the way.

Few racially discriminatory decisions are animated by only one motivation; they typically stem from mixed motives. For example, an employer who prefers white candidates to black candidates—except black candidates with clearly superior experience and test scores—is engaging in racial discrimination, even though race is not the only factor he considers (since he is willing to select black superstars). There are, of course, different degrees of discrimination. In some cases, race is a marginal factor; in others it is the only factor. The distinction may have a bearing on the moral or logical justification for the discrimination. But it cannot logically negate the existence of racial discrimination. Taking race into account at all means engaging in racial discrimination.

Because racial discrimination is discouraged by both law and morality, proponents of racial profiling should bear the burden of persuading the public that such discrimination is justifiable. Instead, defenders of racial profiling frequently neglect the costs of the practice. They unduly minimize (or ignore altogether) the large extent to which racial profiling constantly adds to the sense of resentment felt by blacks of every social stratum toward the law enforcement establishment. Ironically, this is a cost of racial profiling that may well hamper law enforcement. In the immediate aftermath of O.J. Simpson's acquittal, when blacks' accumulated anger at and distrust of the criminal justice system became frighteningly clear, there existed a widespread recognition of the danger that threatens all Americans when cynicism and rage suffuse a substantial sector of the country. Alienation of that sort gives rise to witnesses who fail to cooperate with the police, citizens who view prosecutors as "the enemy," lawyers who disdain the rules they have sworn to uphold, and jurors who yearn to "get even" with a system that has, in their eyes, consistently mistreated them. For the sake of better law enforcement, we need to be mindful of the deep reservoir of anger toward the police that now exists within many racial minority neighborhoods. Racial profiling is a big part of what keeps this pool of accumulated rage filled to the brim.

A Burden on Innocent People

Yet the courts have not been sufficiently mindful of this risk. In the course of rejecting a 1976 constitutional challenge to actions by officers of the U.S. Border Patrol who selected cars for inspection in Southern California partly on the basis of some drivers' apparent Mexican ancestry, the Supreme Court pointed to what it viewed as positive results. The Court noted that, of the motorists passing the checkpoint involved, fewer than one percent were stopped for questioning. It also noted that, of the 820 vehicles inspected pursuant to the profiling during the eight days surrounding the challenged arrests, roughly 20 percent contained illegal aliens.

"The burden placed on innocent people stopped by law enforcement officers because of racial profiling is typically underestimated."

As Justice William J. Brennan noted in dissent, however, the Court provided no indication of the ancestral makeup of all of the persons stopped in conformity with the Border Patrol profile. It is likely that a large percentage of the innocent people who were stopped and questioned were persons of apparent Mexican ancestry who found themselves in the position of having to prove their obedience to the law simply because others of their national origin have engaged in misconduct.

The burden placed on innocent people stopped by law enforcement officers because of racial profiling is typically underestimated. In the case of the Border Patrol, the Supreme Court maintained that the agents' intrusion on those selected for questioning is "quite limited," involving "only a brief detention of travelers during which all that is required . . . is a response to a brief question or two and possibly the production of a document."

There is reason, however, to be skeptical of this upbeat portrait of quick and courteous police intervention. The justices seemed to forget that people who look Mexican and live in border regions are what game theorists call "repeat players." Their national origin, actual or apparent, remains the same long after the first time they get pulled over. Unlike Anglos, Mexicans and Mexican-Americans must contemplate not just the possibility of one or two stops in their lifetimes, but many.

Moreover, everyone involved in such an encounter knows that race played a role in the officer's decision to stop the car, which sets up a downward spiral in relations between the Border Patrol and Latinos. Officers who start out doing their duty courteously will encounter people who resent having been stopped in part because of their racial or national heritage. The people stopped will vent their resentment. The officer will respond in kind, which will provoke the person in the car further. Next thing you know, there's a violent incident. And don't forget that the cops are repeat players in this game, too. How courteous—and how sincerely nonracist—can we expect them to be after a few months of such hassles?

My case against racial profiling concludes on a frankly ideological note. Racial profiling undercuts a good idea that needs more support from both society and the law: that individuals should be judged by public authority on the basis of their own conduct and not on the basis—not even partly on the basis—of racial generalization. Race-dependent policing retards the development and spread of such thinking; indeed, it encourages the opposite tendency.

Racial Equality Is Not Free

What about the fact that in some jurisdictions it is demonstrable that people associated with a given racial group commit a disproportionately large number of the crimes? Our commitment to a just social order should prompt us to end racial profiling even if the generalizations on which the technique is based are buttressed by empirical evidence. This is not as unusual as it may sound. There are actually many contexts in which the law properly enjoins us to forswear the playing of racial odds even when doing so would advance certain legitimate goals.

For example, public opinion surveys have established that blacks tend to be more distrustful than whites of law enforcement. Thus, for purposes of convicting certain defendants, it would be rational—and not necessarily racist—for a prosecutor to use race as a factor in seeking to exclude black potential jurors.

Fortunately, the Supreme Court has outlawed racial discrimination of this sort. Similarly, it is a demographic fact that whites tend to live longer than blacks. Therefore, it would be perfectly rational for insurers to charge blacks higher life-insurance premiums than whites. Fortunately, though, the law forbids that, too. And, given that, statistically, whites tend to be better educated than blacks, it might make business sense for an employer to give a racial edge to white applicants.

> *"Individuals should be judged by public authority on the basis of their own conduct and not on the basis . . . of racial generalization."*

But a battery of laws proscribes racial discrimination in the workplace, even under circumstances in which it would strengthen a business's bottom line.

The point here is that racial equality, like all good things in life, costs something; it does not come for free. Politicians often speak as if all that Americans need to do in order to attain racial justice is forswear bigotry. They must do that. But they must do more as well. They must be willing to demand equal treatment before the law even under circumstances in which unequal treatment is plausibly defensible in the name of nonracist goals. They must even be willing to do so when their effort will be costly.

Responsible Alternatives

Since abandoning racial profiling would undeniably raise the information costs of policing to some extent, with some attendant potential loss in effective crime control, those of us who would do away with it must advocate a responsible alternative. Mine is simply to spend more on other means of enforcement—and then spread the cost on some nonracial basis. This is hardly infeasible. One possibility is hiring more police officers. Another is subjecting everyone to closer surveillance. A benefit of the second option would be to acquaint more whites with the burden of police intrusion, the knowledge of which might prompt more whites to insist upon reining the police in. As it stands now, this burden falls with unfair severity upon minorities—imposing on Mexican-Americans, blacks, and others a special kind of tax for the war against illegal immigration, drugs, and other forms of criminality. The racial character of that tax should be repealed.

I am not saying that police should never be able to refer to race. If a young white man with blue hair robs me, the police should certainly be able to use the description of the perpetrator's race in efforts to apprehend the felon. In this situation, though, whiteness is a trait linked to a particular person with respect to a particular incident. It is not a free-floating proxy for risk that hovers over young white men practically all the time—which is the predicament in which young black men currently find themselves. Nor am I saying absolutely that race could never be legitimately relied upon as a signal of increased danger. In an extraordinary circumstance in which plausible alternatives appear to be absent, officials might appropriately feel bound to resort to racial profiling. This would be right, however, only in a rare instance in which a strong presumption against racial profiling has been overcome by evidence of compelling circumstances. This is a far cry from the situation today, in which racial profiling is routine and is subjected to far less scrutiny than it warrants.

Racial Profiling Should Not Be Abolished

by William Stamps

About the author: *William Stamps is a probation officer in Los Angeles County.*

Since [the terrorist attacks of] September 11 [2001], racial profiling in the United States has taken on new dimensions. As our government tries to search out and bring to justice those responsible for the tragedies, many Americans wonder if the government isn't overextending its legal bounds. In our search for the enemy, are we going too far? Are we sacrificing our sacred and hard-fought-for civil liberties for a few evil men?

Fifty years ago, in certain parts of this country an African American man could be arrested, prosecuted and convicted of a crime for which he was innocent.

Many times it was a simple solution: A scapegoat was needed and who was more "qualified" than a black man? In those days, African Americans were harassed, arrested and falsely accused of crimes without a shred of evidence. There was no limit to how long a black person could be held in custody without charges being filed. Justice was a mockery.

In that era, to have contended that an African American's rights were violated would have been misleading; a black man in America had no rights.

In the pre–civil rights era, African Americans were abused by the police and the justice system solely on the basis of race.

Many were harassed out of hatred, some for sport, others because they were in the wrong place at the wrong time. Many times, there wasn't even an actual crime committed. During some of these judicial proceedings, there wasn't any genuine search for truth and justice; the aim was to harass, abuse and humiliate a race of people because it was acceptable to do so.

Consequently, it is no great surprise that after the civil rights era, racial profiling became a legitimate concern, especially among minorities.

Civil rights attorneys and social activists waged extensive battles with the judicial system to assure that blacks and other minorities who were arrested were afforded the same due process as everyone else.

Arresting and interrogating individuals solely because of their race was no longer acceptable.

An Excellent Investigative Tool

I recall this history to show that it is not a mystery why so many people in the United States are opposed to racial profiling.

Unfortunately, this history has negatively impacted what is otherwise an excellent investigative tool for capturing those who have broken the law. Profiling is a necessary component in any worthwhile criminal investigation. The more information the authorities have on a criminal, the greater the likelihood of capture. Is the suspect young or old? Are the authorities looking for a male or female? Short or tall? Are there any outstanding physical characteristics? Any tattoos?

If all of this is vital and necessary information, why would one exclude race and skin color, if these are known?

Like it or not, race is a necessary component in the overall profile in any criminal investigation. If a pink elephant took peanuts from the peanut jar, I should look for a pink elephant. In my search, I just may confront a few innocent pink elephants before I find the culprit. However, the color of the elephant is vital information to my investigation.

> *"Like it or not, race is a necessary component in the overall profile in any criminal investigation."*

In any criminal investigation, the concern should not be whether individuals fit a certain profile. It should be: Are these individuals being randomly and indiscriminately arrested exclusively based on their race—race being the only factor. The latter is racism. There is a difference.

By screaming racism at every turn, we are only assisting the criminals and hindering law enforcement.

Like everyone else, I love and appreciate our civil liberties. And as a minority, I abhor police injustices to any race of people. However, I don't want to tie the hands of those who make it possible for me to enjoy those liberties.

Our government is in the process of attempting to track down those responsible for the Sept. 11 tragedy.

There are some who would love to hinder this investigation by throwing in as many roadblocks as possible.

There are others whose only agenda is race and they see racism under every rock. Let's allow the U.S. attorney general and other law enforcement personnel to do the job we pay them to do.

Whites Should Examine White Privilege

by Tobin Miller Shearer

About the author: *Tobin Miller Shearer is coauthor of* Set Free: A Journey Toward Solidarity Against Racism, *from which this viewpoint is adapted.*

For most of my adult life, I have been involved in work to overcome racism. For me as a white male, this has meant confronting not only the effects of racism on people of color, but also the ways racism and white privilege have shaped my own life and spirituality.

As I consider racism's effect on my life, I often think of the unnamed scribe in Mark's Gospel who asks Jesus which commandment is the greatest. Jesus surprises the scribe with a twofold response: You shall love the Lord your God with all your heart, soul, mind, and strength; and you shall love your neighbor as yourself. After the scribe affirms Jesus by adding that love of God and neighbor is "much more important than all whole burnt offerings and sacrifices," Jesus tells him: "You are not far from the kingdom of God" (12:28-34).

These words of Jesus ring in my ears, for I think that this scribe's situation parallels the identity of white people who struggle with racism today. Like the scribes of Jesus' time, we are the beneficiaries, the privileged ones in a stratified society that oppresses the poor and defines many as unclean. We are the ones who get "greeted with respect in the marketplace" and have "the best seats in synagogues and places of honor at banquets." By the virtue of our skin color, we end up profiling at the expense of the poor and oppressed.

It is difficult to honestly acknowledge the power and privilege we receive because of our whiteness. Once we do, we may wonder if that is not enough: "Are we really that far from the kingdom?" we ask. "Is something keeping us from entering in?"

We would do well to listen to Jesus' words to the scribe. Even though this exchange is mostly positive—in fact it's the only place in Mark's Gospel where Jesus' interactions with a scribe are not entirely negative—Jesus still does not invite the scribe into the kingdom. He is near, but he is not yet in.

Jesus knows what holds us back from the kingdom. He invites us to enter in.

Confronting White Isolation

To be healthy, all of us need to know who we are. For white people, part of that knowledge comes from recognizing how our whiteness hurts us, how it holds us back. In considering how we might enter the kingdom, I believe there are four "white spaces" we must confront.

The first of these spaces is isolation. Most white people have a difficult time understanding themselves as part of a group. Our first—almost instinctual—response is to think of ourselves as individuals. While this heightened sense of individualism is true of all members of Western society, I believe this impulse tends to be amplified and warped among white people. Many of us have lost any sense of our group identity as white persons.

As I consider the way this dynamic shapes my own life, I see that I sometimes isolate myself from other whites by conveying the impression that I am a well-read, irreproachable antiracist expert. I rationalize that the amount of energy I've devoted to antiracism efforts has earned me the right to no longer acknowledge the effects and reality of racism in my life. I function as if my efforts have somehow separated me from any collective white identity.

Having recognized this tendency, I've begun to try to identify more with the resistance I sometimes experience from other whites in discussions of racism. When I say, "Racism makes all white people into racists," I try to put myself in the place of someone who might be hearing those words for the first time. I remember the resistance I felt when I first heard those words.

It is the same resistance I feel when a colleague of color challenges me about something I have said. It is the same resistance I feel when I realize that I respond differently to the young Latino man who walks past me than I did to the young white man who passed me on the same sidewalk a block earlier.

Long-time antiracism organizer and author Dody Matthias once reminded me, "We have to remember the pain and discomfort we all go through as white people when we first become aware of racism's effects on us. It is like remembering the pain of coming out of the birth canal to look around at a new world."

> *"We [whites] are the beneficiaries, the privileged ones in a stratified society that oppresses the poor and defines many as unclean."*

When I am able to connect with how difficult it is for all of us who are white to name our racism, how difficult it is for each of us to come through that birth canal, I am better able to respond to the resistance I might encounter in a workshop or conversation. I am better able to talk without shame about working against racism in my majority white congregation. And I am ready to stop protecting white people—including myself—from the pain of facing our complicity in this racist system.

In the space of isolation, the task for us is connecting. We who are white are not autonomous individuals. We must learn to understand together that we are a group of people who have all been shaped into being white.

White Control

A second white space is control. For many of us, this may be the most difficult space to visit. We do not want to acknowledge how accustomed we are to being in control. Even when dealing with racism, we want to define the problem and then find the solution, the correct response, to this social evil. We are reluctant to acknowledge the spiritual effects of racism on our lives and our inability to free ourselves completely from its influence.

In institutional settings, the desire for control sometimes takes the form of maintaining and promoting programs that benefit white people at the expense of people of color. Many of the short-term service ventures prevalent in church mission agencies are a prime example of the unspoken desire of white-led institutions to remain in control.

Typically, such programs take privileged and resourced people (most of them white) into impoverished settings for short-term service. In the September 1995 issue of *A Common Place*, James Logan spoke of his experience as a young African American recipient of such short-term service: "I call

> *"We [whites] do not want to acknowledge how accustomed we are to being in control."*

them 'get-to-know-the-ghetto tours.'" Logan points out that such projects contribute to the community's destabilization, rather than increasing its health. "Short-term service is, I think, very much like crack cocaine and alcoholism; it gives a false sense of security. But it does not build a coherent, intergenerational community that empowers its members."

Even in the face of such concerns, short-term service endeavors remain popular. While the effects of such projects are admittedly complex and amorphous, the vast amounts of funding and participation that allow such programs to continue with such vigor seem to indicate that something else is going on. The fact that such service continues to be so prevalent, when that service may in fact be harmful, speaks powerfully of the need for the sponsoring institutions to set the agenda, rather than taking their lead from those in the communities that they seek to serve.

The principal task I've identified in this white space of control is that of letting go. One concrete expression of this is an emphasis on accountability to communities of color. Such accountability can put us in a place of not being able to rely on white privilege.

In our work as an antiracism training team, my colleagues and I try to ensure that people of color get veto power. For example, if one of our workshops includes an uncooperative participant, and we cannot agree whether to confront this person directly or let the behavior go for the time being, we give the people of color the final say. In disagreements over training in potentially volatile settings, again the final word goes to people of color.

I resist strongly being put in situations where I cannot depend on my white control and privilege. Yet I know how powerfully God can act when I allow myself to be grounded in the space of letting go.

White Loss

Racism also situates whites in a place of loss. Yet we who are white seldom recognize what we have lost because of racism, nor are we given permission to grieve this loss.

In the process of becoming white, European Americans lost much of their culture and history. We disowned all intimate understanding of where we came from and how we came to be. We lost our own stories. Just as the people of the Hebrew Scriptures had to remind themselves again and again how they came to be the children of Israel, so do we as white people need to recover our own stories of foundation.

As we begin to confront our own racism, we may be tempted to keep our exploration of these issues on an intellectual level. Confronting issues of race on an emotional and spiritual level can be painful. But if we are open to grieving, we may be able to hear what we have previously ignored.

Author Lillian Roybal Rose has pointed out the need for whites to move beyond a purely intellectual struggling with racism. Yet she recognizes how difficult it will be for most of us: "The movement to a global, ethnic point of view requires tremendous grieving. I encourage white people not to shrink from the emotional content of this process. . . . When the process is emotional as well as cognitive, the state of being an ally becomes a matter of reclaiming one's own humanity."

I suspect that beneath much of our hesitancy to grieve is an emotional response that begs to be expressed— perhaps at first in anger or denial, possibly even in weeping. All these are expressions of grieving the loss of critical, life-giving parts of our humanity. Such grieving takes great courage and commitment. And the importance of a caring and nurturing community to surround us as we grieve cannot be overstated.

> *"We who are white seldom recognize what we have lost because of racism, nor are we given permission to grieve this loss."*

I once witnessed a video of a worldwide gathering of Christian indigenous people. It was filled with images of worship, but it was worship unlike any I had ever experienced. Group after group sang, danced, walked, chanted, and moved in their indigenous dress, language, and style of worship. I saw Maori,

Choctaw, Filipino, Finn, and Zulu worship styles explode with Christ-centered jubilation.

In one scene a middle-aged Indonesian man danced slowly across the screen with a power and grace I have rarely witnessed. As I watched him act out a battle with Satan, his face filled with dignity and strength, I began to cry.

I cried for joy that this fully human, profoundly fleshy experience of worship was still with us. But I also cried out of grief that somewhere in the history of becoming white my own indigenous roots and identity had been left behind. I cried that my mother had been taught that dancing was profound sin. I cried that in my own church congregation we seem to barely register that we even have bodies. And I cried because I knew that as we have called ourselves white and declared ourselves superior, we have also become poorer.

> *"As we have called ourselves white and declared ourselves superior, we have also become poorer."*

If we are willing to be honest with our grief, to confront what we have lost, we can move forward into reclaiming who we are. We can begin to confront our own personal journeys in "becoming white," as well as our family and collective histories. When these tasks of reclamation are undertaken with full knowledge of how the dominant society tries constantly to shape white people into racists, the journey of reclamation can be joyful and life-giving. It can also become a profound act of resistance to racism.

White Self-Loathing

Finally, one of the most curious spaces that racism creates for white people is a space of loathing: both a self-loathing and an active distaste for and mistrust of other white people. I have known some ardently antiracist whites who seem unable to sit down and simply enjoy the company of other white people. It does us no good if, in the midst of working to dismantle racism, we end up hating one another.

Sometimes white people who work to end racism try to express their deep commitment to this cause by lashing out at other white people—or even at themselves. Such attacks are not healthy for us, nor do they help to confront racism. This final white space of loathing must be countered with the difficult task of learning to love ourselves and others.

I was confronted with the difficulty of this at a family reunion one summer. Two of my relatives presented a skit that was introduced as an encounter between a pastor and a "colored" man. The skit proceeded to show a racist stereotype of a confused, illiterate "colored man." complete with Southern drawl.

After getting over our initial shock, my wife Cheryl and I left the room. Amid tears and embarrassment, we talked about how we should respond. We decided that we had to return and say something. Although it was a moment of utter dread and sheer terror, we both felt we could not live with integrity if we did not speak up.

So we went back into that gathering of about one hundred relatives, and spoke about the pain the skit had caused us. I told them how much I want to be proud of my family and described how disappointed and hurt I'd been by our collective silence in the face of the skit. I spoke about how saddened I was by the messages this skit might have taught my young sons. Yet I felt glad that my sons were there to see at least one small way in which we were trying to love each other in spite of this racism.

After we spoke, all I wanted to do was leave. Yet several relatives came up and told me how much they appreciated what Cheryl and I had done. Their presence and support gave me the courage to stay in the room and to continue to be with folks whom I didn't even want to see in those moments.

Loving One Another

It may seem strange to conclude a systemic analysis of the effects of racism on whites by focusing on the interpersonal principle of loving one another. Yet the systemic and the personal are not, in fact, contradictory.

The work of dismantling systemic racism and building new institutions that are not based on white power and privilege needs to be infused with a deep love for and among all of us who are working together. Antiracism work can quickly become warped if it involves white people who fundamentally do not love themselves.

Underlying each of these white spaces—isolation, control, loss, and loathing—is the pattern of internalized superiority that racism has taught all white persons. We have believed that we have the answers. It can shake our very foundations to discover that these lessons of superiority and our ensuing dependence on privilege may inhibit our complete and unlimited entrance to the kingdom.

I believe that our inability to confront and pass through these four white spaces may keep us from completely entering the kingdom. It is my hope that a deeper focus on connection, grounding, reclaiming, and loving might help remove those barriers to living out God's reign that are particular struggles for white people.

Jesus' words to the unnamed scribe serve as both a caution and an invitation. "You are not there yet," he seems to say to us, "but keep working together, so that one day you might all enter the kingdom rejoicing."

Examinations of White Privilege May Be Counterproductive

by Susan Wise Bauer

About the author: *Susan Wise Bauer teaches literature at the College of William and Mary.*

Two years ago, we buried my grandmother in the family graveyard, in the middle of a corn-field. Overtop of the old Confederate soldier graves, the funeral home director set out rows of folding metal chairs for the relatives, and my cousin mowed down the corn around the graveyard's edge so that friends could stand and listen. Just before the minister began the service, a statuesque black woman with a close cap of hair and platform shoes came through the field and sat down at the end of the relatives' row: the only black woman in a cluster of white faces. I didn't recognize her, until my mother leaned forward and whispered. "There's your sister."

My grandmother always gave special presents to my sister, the odd one out, the child who didn't fit. My white parents adopted my sister when she was three days old and I was almost one. She grew up with European features and dark skin, the heritage of her unknown African American father and her teen-aged white mother. We fought all our lives; I was the good girl, while my sister smoked cigarettes, carried on long secretive phone conversations with boys after she was supposed to be in bed, and ignored all the limits my parents set. But I didn't think of our constant bickering as a manifestation of racial tension. She was my sister.

She stopped being my sister sometime in the middle of our college education. At a small Baptist college, she found herself in a militant group of black students who told her that she needed to break the bonds with her white family in order to realize her own black identity. She broke with us: with relief, with joy.

After that I never again had a conversation with her that did not end in race.

Susan Wise Bauer, "Whiteness," *Books & Culture*, vol. 6, September–November 2000, p. 18. Copyright © 2000 by Susan Wise Bauer. Reproduced by permission.

All of our disagreements became crystallized into this single point: You were happy and I wasn't, because you are white and I am black. You're white, and you will never understand. After one particularly spectacular fight, not long after I got married, I stopped calling, stopped writing, stopped trying. We didn't see each other for seven years, until the day she arrived at my grandmother's funeral.

After the ceremony, I told her I was sorry for my own lack of sensitivity. I apologized for ignoring her difficulties as she grew up in a white family. I apologized for trying to force her into my mold.

Afflicted by Whiteness

I apologized for being white. For years, I rejected that relationship-killing accusation: Your Whiteness is a wall between us. After all, I am a person of good will who truly believes that all men and women are made in the image of God. I teach African American authors in my American literature classes. I live in a neighborhood which is mostly black. I pick up black hitchhikers, out here on my country road. My sister is black.

And yet, over the past few years, I've begun to realize that something is adrift in my life. I have few black friends; my rural church is entirely white; my immediate neighbors are white; I rarely have a black student in my American literature classes. In

> *"'Whiteness studies' exploded in the 1990s, fueled by a growing discontent with the de facto segregation of American university campuses."*

my eagerness to demonstrate my lack of prejudice, I find myself reacting to the African American clerk in the drugstore, the housekeeping staff at the university, the black linguistics professor down the hall, with the insincerity that W.E.B. Du Bois chronicled with deadly perception in his 1903 classic, *The Souls of Black Folk:*

> Between me and the other world there is ever an unasked question: unasked by some through feelings of delicacy; by others through the difficulty of rightly framing it. All, nevertheless, flutter round it. They approach me in a half-hesitant sort of way, eye me curiously or compassionately, and then, instead of saying directly, How does it feel to be a problem? they say, I know an excellent colored man in my own town . . . or, Do not these Southern outrages make your blood boil? At these I smile, or am interested . . . as the occasion may require. To the real question, How does it feel to be a problem? I answer seldom a word.

A hundred years later, I find myself uttering the same words, updated; Doesn't the whole South Carolina confederate-flag thing drive you crazy? Or, By the way, my sister is black. I grope awkwardly—and unsuccesfully—to make a connection, to say without using the words: I see you as a human being. I reject racism. I am not prejudiced.

I behave, in fact, like any well-educated, good-intentioned, middle-class woman afflicted by Whiteness.

Whiteness Studies

In the last two years I've become increasingly willing to consider the part Whiteness plays in my life. Not coincidentally, I've also spent the last two years finishing my Ph.D. in American Studies. Whiteness was born in academia: "Whiteness studies" exploded in the 1990s, fueled by a growing discontent with the de facto segregation of American university campuses. African American Studies departments study black America, but don't have much interaction with the history and religion departments that are scrutinizing white America. Black students flee from "regular" literature courses and enroll in courses on black literature, taught by black faculty. Amiable middle-class college students, raised to understand that any display of prejudice is in bad taste, nevertheless eat, sleep, and entertain themselves apart.

University cafeterias are the showplace for this voluntary ghettoization: "There's a sea of pink and peach faces . . . all gathered around the front tables by the salad bar," observes Princeton Theological Seminary student Sarah Hinlicky in *First Things*. "Look farther back and at the other end of the room, by the cereal and the back door, all the brown and black faces together." Despite the civil rights revolution, the last wall between the races—the social wall—remains thick and high.

White students, knowing their own good will, have felt that the segregation is voluntary. "It's embarrassing, like Rosa Parks on the bus, except the other way around," Hinlicky writes. "We don't care to sit in the front with you, thanks, we'll retreat to the back on our own." But scholars of race, unhappy with a solution that shifts the blame onto students of color, have come up with another explanation. Whites have made it impossible for students of color to take full part in university culture—not by acting prejudiced, but simply by acting white.

For those who have difficulty wrapping their brains around the concept of Whiteness. Unitarian theologian Thandeka suggests the Race Game. The Game has only one rule: use the term "white" whenever you mention the name of a European American friend or relative, as in "My white husband John told me . . ." Thandeka invented the Race Game when a white colleague of hers at Smith College asked her, over lunch, what it felt like to be black "I guaranteed her," she writes in *Learning to be White: Money, Race and God in America*, "that if she played the Race Game for a week and then met me for lunch, I

> *"Whiteness studies aims to . . . [make] the 'unspoken' racial identity of whites obvious."*

could answer her question using terms she would understand. We never had lunch together again. Apparently my suggestion had made her uncomfortable."

This discomfort, Thandeka explains, comes from the nature of Whiteness; it is the racial identity which never has to speak its name. "Whiteness" is the invisible norm against which all other cultural groups are defined. Among all racial groups—African-American, Native American, Hispanic American, Asian American—only whites are "assumed not to 'have race,'" observes David Roediger, one of the leading theorists of Whiteness. American culture, George Lipsitz writes, is "obviously white culture"; to speak of the "American people" is to imply white people, unless a qualifier is inserted (as in "the black vote"). Mainstream America is white; Benjamin Franklin, Emily Dickinson, and John Grisham are at the center, while Frederick Douglass and Frances Harper are sideshows. ("What about Oprah?" is not, according to scholars of race, an appropriate question to ask at this point.)

> *"According to race scholars, the non-experience of Whiteness is . . . something rather sinister."*

Whiteness is responsible for the cafeteria separation, because black students, cast in among whites, feel the pressure of an invisible unspoken norm and retreat from it, creating enclaves within which they are the norm and whites are the outsiders. Whiteness studies aims to break down this impasse by making the "unspoken" racial identity of whites obvious. All Americans, not just minorities, have a racial identity that shapes them. The first commandment of Whiteness studies, coming before all others, is: Recognize that you are not colorless; you are the color white. And the second, like unto the first, is: Your color has distorted your view of the world. . . .

Shaping Racial Identity

Unlike blackness, Whiteness isn't obvious to those who have been raised in it. White children are brought up to believe that white is, simply, normal; being white is, in Geoffrey Fowler's words, a "non-experience." But according to race scholars, the non-experience of Whiteness is, in fact, something rather sinister. White children, writes Thandeka, are all "socialized into a system of values that holds in contempt differences from the white community's ideals." The price of Whiteness is the rejection of all non-white emotions, ways of knowing, traditions, and interpretations of history.

Although nonwhites can identify this massive unspoken prejudice, naming it for what it is, the only way America can break her racial stalemate—so the Whiteness theorists say—is for white people to recognize and reject their invisible racial identity. A massive re-education program is America's only hope. But who is qualified to take on the enormous job of guiding an entire generation into a new way of thinking?

Why, university administrators and faculty, of course; those same folks who are currently presiding over the cafeterias where whites and blacks eat on opposite sides of the room.

College has long been a place where racial identities are provided to young, passionate people who weren't aware that their identities were incomplete. At university, my sister learned that she could be black and free herself from her white family. Scores of memoirs record the same phenomenon.

In *Beyond the Whiteness of Whiteness: A Memoir of a White Mother of Black Sons*, Jane Lazarre describes her upbringing in "the subculture of the American Left," where she was taught that "slavery and racism sit at the heart of American experience, a cruel mockery of the idea and practice of democracy." Lazarre, a Jewish woman, had two sons with her African American husband and raised them with care and sensitivity. So she was legitimately startled when her son Khary came home from his first year of college and explained repeatedly to his mother that he was not biracial, not Jewish, but black. "He goes on to explain his beliefs and feelings in detail." Lazarre writes, "and when I say, 'I understand,' he tells me carefully, gently, 'I don't think you do, Mom. You can't understand this completely because you're white.'"

Though saddened, Lazarre is willing to accept that the university knows best:

> At first, I am slightly stunned, by his vehemence and by the idea. . . . I have used the experience of motherhood to try to comprehend the essential human conflict between devotion to others and obligations to the self. . . . Now, standing in a darkened hallway facing my son, I feel exiled from my not-yet-grown child. . . . What is this Whiteness that threatens to separate me from my own child? Why haven't I seen it lurking, hunkering down, encircling me in some irresistible fog?

With the help of her college-educated sons, Lazarre begins to understand the part that Whiteness has played in her well-intentioned life. Even her progressive upbringing, she writes, is part of her "miseducation as a white American."

In the PBS documentary *American Love Story*, another mixed family spends a year in front of the camera: Bill and Karen, black and white, have lived together for 20 years, been married for a decade, and are raising two light-skinned black daughters. In Episode 3, oldest daughter Cicely goes off to Colgate after a childhood in which she was taught to think of herself as an individual, not black or white. "When I see other kids who are biracial, or multiracial families" she tells the camera, "I see people who are totally Afrocentric or who want to be white. And they're just really messed up. I am Cicely." But she doesn't get through college without facing up to her racial identity. "That answer would have done," she muses, "that was sufficient for me through high school and the first year of college. But now: I am still Cicely, but I am multiracial as well."

> *"No matter how much good will you find in yourself, if you're an American of European ancestry, you have been corroded by Whiteness."*

Cicely tries to include both black and white students within her circle of friends but finds herself continually pressured to reject her white heritage in order to be "fully black." Her Colgate classmates, interviewed by filmmaker Jennifer Fox, are emphatic: "You have to choose," Edwin tells us. He's a heavy, intense boy, speaking straight to the camera. "If you want to be down, you have to choose that you are black.

The line had to be drawn. You have to be down with us or not down with us. You have to be one or the other. You couldn't be both." His own coffee-with-cream skin shows clear evidence of white heritage, but the irony is apparently lost on him. . . .

Cicely, who takes up smoking halfway through Episode 3 and has a cigarette in her hand for most of the interviews that follow, finds this pressure to choose almost unendurable. "I wasn't really friends with the black community at Colgate," she says gloomily. "They think I'm an ignorant person trying to be white or something, you know. . . . Maybe I was brought up in an idealistic household. Maybe that's affecting me now."

> *"The strategies of Whiteness re-education have not, so far, set college campuses on fire with reconciliation."*

Cicely and Khary are both at least half white, but the black community around them rejects any claim they might lay to Whiteness; this would be a pretense, "trying to be white." Cicely's white friends think that she is suffering because of the inflexibility of the black students. "It seems," one of her white Colgate classmates says, tentatively, "that a lot of the tension came from the black students . . . not the white students."

The Re-Education of White Students

It might seem reasonable to approach black students about this tension created by an iron-fisted insistence on absolute racial identity. But universities, influenced by the growing field of Whiteness studies, have instead chosen to focus their re-education efforts on white students. After all, blacks have simply internalized the white-created definition of race: Whiteness is that which excludes all blackness, so all students with any African blood must be black.

The re-education begins even before classes start. White, middle-class freshmen, arriving at orientation ready to learn about meal plans and the dubious authority of resident assistants, are also treated to sensitivity exercises about their Whiteness. This trend, notes Heather MacDonald in the *Wall Street Journal*, stems from the university's conviction that freshmen need

> political re-education. Columbia's assistant dean for freshmen, Kathryn Balmer, explained that "you can't bring all these people together and say, 'Now be one big happy community,' without some sort of training. . . . It isn't an ideal world, so we need to do some education." This education enlightens students about their white racial identity, and then encourages them to "acknowledge oneself as the oppressor."

In "Thought Reform 101," Alan Charles Kors chronicles this university reprogramming:

> At Wake Forest University [in the fall of 1999], one of the few events designated as "mandatory" for freshman orientation was attendance at *Blue Eyed*, a

filmed racism awareness workshop in which whites are abused, ridiculed, made to fail, and taught helpless passivity so that they can identify with "a person of color for a day." In Swarthmore College's dormitories, in the fall of 1998, first-year students were asked to line up by skin color, from lightest to darkest, and to step forward and talk about how they felt concerning their place in that line. [This orientation assumes that] white students desperately need formal "training" in racial and cultural awareness. . . . [They] "have to be trained as allies. [A]n "ally" is someone from "the dominant group" who is aware of and articulates his unmerited privilege.

This re-education of white students excludes no one. Kors writes that sensitivity instructor Jane Elliot (producer of *Blue Eyed*) began a lecture at Kansas State University by explaining that "all whites are racists, whatever they believe about themselves: 'If you want to see another racist, turn to the person on your right. Now look at the person on your left.'"

No matter how much good will you find in yourself, if you're an American of European ancestry, you have been corroded by Whiteness.

> *"White students . . . are offered no option but to live forever in a state of ongoing abject repentance, with guilt as an ever-present roommate."*

Does re-education work? Have universities become the birthplace of a new America, one where racial divisions begin to lose their hard edges because whites admit their part in creating racial identities? Sensitivity exercises have been commonplace on American campuses since at least 1996. How do the cafeterias look now?

Well, pretty much like they did before scholars of Whiteness set their re-education program in motion.

The Sin of Whiteness

The strategies of Whiteness re-education have not, so far, set college campuses on fire with reconciliation. But this should not surprise anyone with a rudimentary knowledge of human psychology—since this re-education binds a bagload of guilt on the backs of White students, without providing any convenient cross for them to drop it at.

The language of Whiteness is, more often than not, explicitly religious. "There is some burden we must bear by being white Americans," Jane Lazarre writes, describing the original sin of Whiteness. "I have been born into color." But beyond this flawed identity, there is hope for Whites who are willing to admit their participation in the original sin. Whiteness is "a burden which can be redemptive, not oppressive"—but only if white Americans are willing to be born again.

This rebirth is "into a consciousness of color. . . . Being born means . . . the development of knowledge over time." The new birth Lazarre suggests is a birth into a new way of thinking, and it has the power to change her very identity; she is no longer White, but something else. She concludes the story of her rebirth:

> In all racialized situations, that is to say all situations in which Black people and white people who are not on close, personal terms find themselves together, I am always comforted by this thought: I am no longer white. However I may appear to others, I am a person of color now. . . . Some color with no precise name.

What race scholars offer to well-intentioned whites is the equivalent of a religious conversion: Move from one identity to another. Shuck off the old man, put on the new. Admit that you wronged all non-Whites by your very existence. Society will be changed by White admission of guilt, and by White acceptance of a new central story around which Whites can build new lives.

But practically speaking, this admission of White guilt is made nearly impossible—because no atonement can ever be made for the sin of Whiteness. Unitarian theologian and race scholar Thandeka, psychoanalyzing [Christian theorist] Bill McCartney (from a distance), explicitly rejects the Christian theology of atonement for guilt by using McCartney as a paradigmatic Christian:

> Writes McCartney: "We've stood against a lot of other social evils, but we have not stood against racism and called it what it is: sin! . . . We should drop to our knees before Almighty God in repentance." McCartney, by transforming his feelings of shame into a recognition of white guilt for the sin of white racism, has turned both white racism and his own white racial identity into an affair that can be handled only by God and his Son. . . . What remains is a man with a white racial self-identity desensitized to his own unresolved feelings from the painful awareness of his complicity in racist acts. Such a man emerges from this process with an arrogant Christian self-assurance.

Nor is there much prospect of forgiveness from those who have been wronged. Unlike the Christian confession, made before God in assurance of forgiveness, the confession of complicity in Whiteness is a horizontal one, made before nonwhites—and if you're White, nonwhites (at least the ones encountered during freshmen orientations) are furious at you. The widely used college orientation film *Skin Deep* is, in the words of Alan Kors, a

> 1996 film funded by the Ford Foundation [that] records an encounter at a retreat between college students from around the country. . . . We meet white, Hispanic, black, and Asian-American students from the University of Massachusetts at Amherst, the University of California at Berkeley, and Texas A&M. . . . When white students initially suggest that they personally did not do terrible things, the students of color fire back with both barrels. A first reply goes immediately to the heart of the matter: "One thing that you must definitely understand is that we're discussing how this country was founded, and because you are a white male, people are going to hate you.". . . The Chicana, Judy, lets them know that "I will not stop being angry, and I will not be less angry or frustrated to accommodate anybody. You whites have to understand because we have been oppressed for 2,000 years. And if you take offense, so?"

White students who admit their complicity in Whiteness are offered no option but to live forever in a state of ongoing abject repentance, with guilt as an ever-present roommate. . . .

Race-Thinking Is Destructive

It is difficult for a white person (like myself) to object to racial identity as a category; unlike an African-American or Hispanic believer. I have nothing to gain and a great deal to lose from accepting a racial identity. But fortunately there are more distinguished voices joining me. The most prominent is probably that of Paul Gilroy, an impeccably credentialed black scholar, professor of sociology and African American Studies at Yale, author of *The Black Atlantic* and *There Ain't No Black in the Union Jack.* Gilroy's most recent book, *Against Race: Imagining Political Culture Beyond the Color Line*, argues that racial identity pushes us further and further apart. "Race-thinking," Gilroy suggests, has "the power to destroy any possibility of human mutuality and cosmopolitan democracy."

The dismantling of racial identity is an unpopular project, Gilroy admits; both whites ("beneficiaries of racial hierarchy [who] do not want to give up their privileges") and blacks ("people who have been subordinated by race-thinking and its distinctive social structures" but have used race-thinking nonetheless to build "complex traditions of politics, ethics, identity and culture") have a great deal invested in the maintenance of the color-line. But the gains are an illusion: blacks and whites both lose from race-thinking, which "estrange[s] them from each other and amputate[s] their common humanity."

Reading Gilroy, I was suddenly aware of how long it had been since I thought of my sister without her race central in my mind. When I spoke of her to others, I identified her as black, in an attempt to make her concerns and difficulties real to them. And in doing so, I had cut her off; all of her personality, her preoccupations, her disappointments and her fears, became not hers, but black. I had fallen into the trap of race-thinking.

Gilroy, unlike Whiteness scholars, proposes a solution: we should replace the category of race with a "pragmatic, planetary humanism" based on "an abstract sense of a human similarity powerful enough to make solidarities based on cultural particularity appear

"Blacks and whites both lose from race-thinking."

suddenly trivial." And here I must part company with Gilroy, who several times contrasts his brand of utopian thinking with the traditional Christian belief in an otherworldly Kingdom. Christianity, he suggests more than once, hampered black efforts to "address the future" because "Black Christianity had been rooted in the belief that the only habitable future lay in another, better world beyond this valley of dry bones."

This dubious characterization of black Christianity as completely focused on another world ignores a substantial body of scholarship arguing that Christianity instead served as an impetus for social reform. Yet there is a sense in which Gilroy is right about the difference between his "planetary humanism" and the Christian world-view. For Gilroy, the core of "planetary humanism" is the will to shape our own destiny, and the corresponding freedom to do so. But as Stanley Hauerwas warns us in *After Christendom*, this power over our future and the autonomy that the human race claims as necessary to shape the future are not compatible with the life pictured in the gospel:

> For the salvation promised in the good news is not a life free from suffering, free from servitude, but rather a life that freely suffers, that freely serves, because such suffering and service is the hallmark of the Kingdom established by Jesus. . . . We have learned that freedom cannot be had by becoming "autonomous"—free from all claims except those we voluntarily accept—but rather freedom literally comes by having our self-absorption challenged by the needs of another.

Gilroy's free futuristic humans and the members of the Kingdom I inhabit are potentially at odds; both may reject race-thinking, but they are likely to come to very different conclusions about what should replace it. Ultimately, the communal identity we must build to replace Blackness and Whiteness is centered around the church: a community which does indeed (in the words of Geoffrey Fowler) define who we are and charge us with the responsibility to work for its good.

The next time I talk to my sister, I will not apologize for my Whiteness. I have plenty of real sins to apologize for: my lack of patience, my failures in humility and in kindness, my arrogance, my willingness to manipulate a younger sibling into doing things my way. I'll start there.

Americans Should Prepare Themselves for Increasing Racial Diversity

by Farai Chideya

About the author: *Farai Chideya is the author of* The Color of Our Future.

America is facing the largest cultural shift in its history. Around the year 2050, whites will become a "minority." This is uncharted territory for this country, and this demographic change will affect everything. Alliances between the races are bound to shift. Political and social power will be re-apportioned. Our neighborhoods, our schools and workplaces, even racial categories themselves will be altered. Any massive social change is bound to bring uncertainty, even fear. But the worst crisis we face today is not in our cities or neighborhoods, but in our minds. We have grown up with a fixed idea of what and who America is, and how race relations in this nation work. We live by two assumptions: that "race" is a black and white issue, and, that America is a "white" society. Neither has ever been strictly true, and today these ideas are rapidly becoming obsolete.

Just examine the demographic trends. In 1950, America was nearly 85 percent non-Hispanic white. Today, this nation is 73 percent non-Hispanic white, 12 percent black, 11 percent Hispanic, 3 percent Asian and 1 percent Native American. (To put it another way, we're about three-quarters "white" and one-quarter "minority.") But America's racial composition is changing more rapidly than ever. The number of immigrants in America is the largest in any post-World War II period. Nearly one-tenth of the U.S. population is foreign born. Asian Americans, the fastest-growing group in America, have begun to come of age politically in California and the Pacific Northwest (where a Chinese American is governor of Washington State). And the Census projects that the Latino Americans will surpass blacks as the largest "minority" group by 2005.[1]

---

1. Hispanics surpassed blacks as the largest minority group in 2003.

Farai Chideya, "A Nation of Minorities: America in 2050," *Civil Rights Journal*, vol. 4, Fall 1999, p. 34.

Yet our idea of "Americanness" has always been linked with "whiteness," from tales of the Pilgrims forward. We still see the equation of white=American every day in movies and on television (where shows like *Mad About You*, set in majority-"minority" New York, have no nonwhite main characters). We witness it in the making of social policy. (The U.S. Senate is only 4 percent nonwhite—though over 20 percent of the country is.) We make casual assumptions about who belongs in this society and who is an outsider. (Just ask the countless American-born Asians and Latinos who've been complimented on how well they speak English.)

Media-Driven Images

"Whiteness" would not exist, of course, without something against which to define itself. That thing is "blackness." Slavery was the forging crucible of American racial identity, setting up the black/white dichotomy we have never broken free from. The landmarks of American history are intimately intertwined with these racial conflicts—the Civil War, Jim Crow, the Civil Rights movement. But today, even as America becomes more diverse, the media still depicts the world largely in black and white. The dramas and sitcoms we watch are so segregated that the top-10 shows in black households and the top-10 shows in white households barely overlap. Or examine the news media. The three-year long coverage of the O.J. Simpson trials portrayed a nation riven by the black/white color line. And when *Nightline* did a first-rate series on race, it still didn't cover the true range of diversity but "America in Black and White." Race is almost always framed as bipolar—the children of slaves vs. the children of slaveowners—even when the issues impact Asians, Latinos and Native Americans as well. School segregation, job integration—they're covered in black and white. Political rivalries, dating trends, income inequalities—they're covered as two-sided dilemmas as well.

Everyone gets exposed to media images of race. Kids who have never met an African American will learn about slavery in school, listen to rap or R & B, and read an article on welfare reform or the NBA. It's only human nature to put together those pieces and try to synthesize an idea of what it means to be "black." The media and pop culture have such a tremendous power in our society because we use them to tell us what the rest of the society is like, and how we should react to it. The problem is that, too often, the picture we're getting is out of kilter.

> *"If you're not black and not white, you're not very likely to be seen."*

If you're not black and not white, you're not very likely to be seen. According to a study by the Center for Media and Public Affairs, the proportion of Latino characters on prime-time television actually dropped from 3 percent in the 1950s to 1 percent in the 1980s, even as the Latino population rapidly grew. Asian Americans are even harder to find in entertainment, news, or on the national agenda, and Native Americans rarer still. How we perceive race, and how it's depicted in print and on television, has less to do with demographic reality than our mindset. National opinion polls reveal that, in the basest and most stereotypic terms, white Americans are considered "true" Americans; black Americans are considered inferior Americans; Asians and Latinos are too often considered foreigners; and Native Americans are rarely thought of at all.

The Millennium Generation

The media's stereotypic images of race affect all of us, but especially the young Americans who are just beginning to form their racial attitudes. I call the young Americans coming of age today the Millennium Generation. These 15–25 year olds are the most racially mixed generation this nation has ever seen—the face of the new America. As a group, they are 60 percent more likely to be nonwhite than their parent and grandparent generations, those American Baby Boomers aged 35 and older. No less than one-third of young Americans aged 15 to 25 are black, Latino, Asian or Native American. While the older generations largely rely on the media to provide them with images of a multi-ethnic America, this generation is already living in it.

The teens and twenty-somethings of the Millennium Generation are the true experts on the future of race, because they're re-creating America's racial identity every single day. They're more likely to interact with people of other races and backgrounds than other generations, and they've grown up seeing multi-ethnic images. Critically important, a third of this generation is nonwhite, not just black but Asian, Latino, Native American and multiracial. Yet the rhetoric which they hear about race dashes abruptly with the realities of their lives. 1990s-style conservatism (led by the "Republican Revolution" which swept Congress in 1994) has included a healthy dollop of anti-immigration and anti-multicultural rhetoric. Politicians (and parents) of every political persuasion tend to cast the race debate in black and white, but the truth of this generation's lives is far more complex and colorful.

"The media's stereotypic images of race affect all of us, but especially the young Americans who are just beginning to form their racial attitudes."

The members of the Millennium Generation defy the easy racial stereotypes. Take an issue as heated as illegal immigration—and the life of an Oakland teen named Diana. Serious and thoughtful, with hopes of going on to college, the Mexican immigrant has lived most of her life in California. She's more familiar with American culture (not to mention more articulate in English) than most teens. But she doesn't have a green card, and her chances of pursuing her college dreams seem slim. Her dad has a green card and two of her four siblings are U.S. citizens because they were born in the United States. Diana was born in Mexico. So, even though she came to the U.S. at the age of two, Diana will have a nearly impossible time getting citizenship unless she finds the money to hire an immigration lawyer to fight her case. It would be easy to think of Diana as some kind of anomaly, but she's not. Countless undocumented immigrants have spent the majority of their lives in this country. And in California alone, there are over a million

> *"Eighty percent of teens have a close friend of another race."*

residents who belong to families of mixed immigration status. Another flashpoint is the battle over affirmative action. Berkeley student LaShunda Prescott could be portrayed as a case of affirmative action gone awry, a black student admitted to a school she wasn't ready for. An engineering student, LaShunda dropped out of Berkeley twice before graduating. But during that time she looked out for a drug-addicted sister, took care of one of the sister's children, and dealt with the death of one family member and the shooting of another. In context, her circuitous route through college is not a failure but a triumph.

LaShunda's schoolmate Steve Mohebi shows another side of the new racial dilemmas. The vice president of the Berkeley College Republicans, he defends, even promotes, recruiting in fraternities where "minorities are not welcome." What's new is not the sentiment, but the fact that Steve himself isn't even white. Nor is he black. He's Middle Eastern, a Persian immigrant. The lives of people like Diana, LaShunda and Steve are compass points on a map of America's complex social terrain. If we want to understand where America is headed, we've got to take a look at where this generation is today—and how they differ from the generations of the past.

A Splintering Divide

Young Americans like these illustrate a fault line in the race debates that most of us don't even think about: a massive generation gap. On the one hand, America is led by Baby Boomers and people from the generations that came before them. These movers and shakers in government and industry came of age before and during the Civil Rights era, while America was dealing with (and reeling from) the struggles of blacks to gain legal equality with whites. When they grew up, America was much whiter, both demographically and culturally. The most powerful images of the era show the divide. The top movies and television shows excluded blacks, and our archives are filled with photographs of black and white youth during the Civil Rights Era, such as the stormy desegregation of Little Rock High.

On the other hand, Americans in their teens and twenties are coming of age at a time which seems less momentous than the Civil Rights Era, but is even more complex. This generation sees firsthand evidence in their own schools and neighborhoods that America is becoming less white and more racially mixed. Yet the court battles of today aren't over providing legal equality for African

Americans; they're about whether to keep or end programs like affirmative action, which were set up to achieve civil rights goals. The cultural battles loom even larger than the legal ones, from the debate over multiculturalism on campus to issues like inter-racial dating. America's pop culture today is infinitely more likely to show blacks as well as whites (though other races often remain unseen). The billion-dollar hip hop industry, produced by blacks but driven by sales to young fans of all races, is one indicator of the cultural shift. Even more significant, eighty percent of teens have a close friend of another race.

Young Americans today aren't just on one side of a generation gap. They ARE a generation gap, the core of a massive transition. America has been a majority-white nation obsessed with black and white issues. And America is becoming a "majority-minority" nation with a multi-racial and multi-cultural population. The problem is that, in some ways, we're neither here nor there. We haven't left the first model behind, nor fully embraced the second. A moment emblematic of the tensions between the black/white and multi-ethnic views of America occurred in 1997, when President Bill Clinton convened a seven-member advisory board on race relations. One of the members, Korean American attorney Angela Oh, announced that she thought the board shouldn't waste too much time analyzing slavery and race relations via "the black-white paradigm." "We need to go beyond that, because the world is about much more than that," she said. "We can't undo this part of our heritage. But what we can affect is where we are headed." Oh is in her early forties and grew up in Los Angeles, a multi-racial city with strong ties to Asia, Mexico and Latin America. She became a spokesperson for Korean shopkeepers looted after the Rodney King verdict, and serves on the Los Angeles Human Rights Commission. Even though she's a Baby Boomer, she grew up in one of the nation's most multi-ethnic enclaves, and thinks along those lines.

> *"A study by the National Opinion Research Center found that the majority of whites still believe blacks to be inferior."*

But esteemed African American historian John Hope Franklin, professor emeritus at Duke University, responded sharply to Oh's request. "This country cut its eye teeth on black-white relations. Without knowledge of the past, we cannot wisely chart our course for the future," he said. Franklin was born in Oklahoma in 1915. Unlike Oh, he's seen Jim Crow and the Civil Rights movement firsthand.

A Multi-Colored Future

Of course, Franklin and Oh are both right. No one can deny that slavery created both racial income inequalities and the American concept of "blackness" (including the stereotypes of intellectual inferiority) which exist to this day. But we can't think that studying black and white relations alone will give us the keys to a better future. That future will come in many colors, not in monochrome. But we can't forget the economic disparities between blacks and whites during this time of transition. Many blacks and whites fear (with some justification) that in a "multi-racial" America, blacks will simply be pushed to the bottom of a bigger barrel. It doesn't help matters that America's non-white groups have so much trouble learning to cooperate. In cities as far flung as New York, Washington, Houston, Chicago, Los Angeles and Oakland, there have been tensions between Latinos and blacks, or blacks and Asians, or all three groups at once. In Houston and Oakland, blacks and Latinos battled for control of the school systems; in Los Angeles and New York, blacks and Asians warred over who should profit from shops in the 'hood. But Mexican Americans have joined blacks as scapegoats of the affirmative action wars, and Asians have joined the ranks of those most targeted for hate crimes. While all of these groups are battling each other, they're ignoring one important fact: they're all the common enemy of people who think that one day soon, America will become "too" non-white.

> *"Most Americans know little about the profound differences separating the income, health and educational opportunities of Americans of different races."*

The very idea that America will become "majority-minority" scares the hell out of some people. That's why we find ourselves not only at a point of incredible change, but of incredible fear. The 1990s have seen a full-scale backlash against immigrants and non-whites, both in word and in deed. As the visibility of non-whites has been rising, hate crimes have too—with attacks on increasingly visible Latinos and Asian Americans rising the fastest. Over the 1999 Fourth of July weekend, a white supremacist named Benjamin Nathaniel Smith went on a shooting spree in Illinois, killing an African American and an Asian American, and wounding another Asian American and six Orthodox Jews. But extremists like Smith are not the only Americans clinging to prejudices. A study by the National Opinion Research Center found that the majority of whites still believe blacks to be inferior (with smaller numbers holding the same views of Southern whites and Hispanics).

The Policy Backlash

The biggest backlash has been in America's policy arena. In 1997, the U.S. Congress passed and President Bill Clinton signed restrictions not just on illegal but legal immigrants. (For example, many legal immigrants are no longer eligible for government medical care.) The debate over affirmative action has turned ugly, with opponents like University of Texas law professor Lino Graglia stating that "blacks and Mexican Americans are not academically competitive with whites" because of "a culture that seems not to encourage achievement." (He later added: "I don't know that it's good for whites to be with the lower classes. I'm afraid it may actually have deleterious effect on their views because they will see people from situations of economic deprivation usually behave less attractively.") Sadly, even the basic tenets of the Civil Rights movement are still controversial. Take Supreme Court Justice Antonin Scalia's response when asked by a law professor how he would have ruled on the *Brown v. Board of Education* case which ended legal segregation. Scalia pondered for a moment—then said he might well have decided in favor of the segregated school system.

The halls of power in America are still segregated. Many corporations and even government agencies look much like they did half a century ago, before Martin Luther King, Jr. marched to Selma, [Alabama]. Ninety-five percent of corporate management—the presidents, vice presidents, and CEOs who run America—are white males. Or as *Newsweek*'s article put it: "White males make up just 39.2 percent of the population, yet they account for 82.5 percent of the Forbes 400 (folks worth at least $265 million), 77 percent of Congress, 92 percent of state governors, 70 percent of tenured college faculty, almost 90 percent of daily-newspaper editors, 77 percent of TV news directors." The image of a hostile takeover of America by non-white guerrilla forces is patently a lie.

> *"Instead of attacking the problems of race, we seem intent on attacking the non-white races."*

What remains a sad truth is the racial divide in resources and opportunity. The unemployment rate is one good indicator. For decades, the black unemployment rate has been approximately twice that of whites. In 1995, the unemployment rate was 3.3 percent for whites, 6.6 percent for blacks, 5.1 percent for Hispanics, and 3.2 percent for Asian Americans.

Recent polls indicate that most Americans know little about the profound differences separating the income, health and educational opportunities of Americans of different races. This makes a profound difference in how we think of racial issues. In a series of polls, Americans who believed that the opportunities and incomes of blacks and whites were equal were much less likely to support programs to end racial discrepancies. Too many of us try to wish the problem of race away instead of confronting it. Instead of attacking the problems of race, we seem intent on attacking non-white races, including those members of the next generation who belong to "minority" ethnic groups.

Paths for the Future

We have better options than tearing each other apart. Instead of fearing the change in American society, we can prepare for it. Here are some simple suggestions:

• *Know the Facts About America's Diversity.* Evaluate how much you know about race in America. According to an array of surveys, white Americans—who at this moment in time make up over three-quarters of the adult population—have an inaccurate view of the racial opportunity gap. Those misperceptions then contribute to their views on issues like the need for the government to address racial inequality.

• *Demand Better Media Coverage of Race.* One study which tracked a year's worth of network news coverage found that sixty percent of images of blacks were negative, portraying victims, welfare dependents and criminals. That is a far cry from the reality about the black community. The news and even the entertainment we read, listen to and watch has a tremendous influence on our perception of societal problems.

> *"The real test of our strength will be how willing we are to go beyond the narrowness of our expectations [and] seek knowledge about the lives of those around us."*

• *Foster Coalitions Between Non-White Groups.* Particularly in urban areas, it's becoming increasingly likely that various non-white groups will share the same community. For example, South Asians and Latinos live next to each other in parts of Queens, New York, and Blacks, Latinos, and Asians share the same neighborhood in Oakland, California. But even though blacks, Latinos, Asians and Native Americans often share common issues, they don't have a good track record of joining together. Every city has groups trying to make a difference. One example is Los Angeles's MultiCultural Collaborative, a group of Korean, Latino and black grassroots organizers formed in response to the destruction following the Rodney King verdict.

• *Foster Coalitions Between Whites and Non-Whites.* Just as important as forming coalitions between different nonwhite groups is changing the often antagonistic politics between the racial majority (whites) and racial "minorities." One way of doing this is to bring together like-minded groups from different communities. For example, the Parent-Teacher Association from a majority-black school could meet with the PTA from a mostly-Asian school, to discuss their common goals, specific challenges, and how they might press government officials to improve education in their district.

• *Demand "Color Equality" Before "Color Blindness."* Segregation is still a pervasive problem in American society, most of all for blacks but for virtually every other race as well. But does that mean we should attempt to overcome segregation and bias by demanding a "color blind" society—one where we talk less, think less, and certainly act without regard to race. The term "color blind" has become increasingly popular, but it avoids a couple of fundamental truths. If racial inequality is a problem, it's terribly difficult to deal with the problem by simply declaring we're all the same. Moreover, do we want to be the same, or equal? Who, for example, could envision New York without a Chinatown and a Little Italy?

• *Re-Desegregate the School System.* Four decades after the *Brown v. Board of Education* ruling, over sixty percent of black students still attend segregated schools. In many municipalities, the statistics are getting worse, not better. The Supreme Court has consistently ruled in the past decade that even strategies like creating magnet programs in mostly-minority schools could not be used as a desegregation strategy. It would be nothing less than a tragedy if at the precise moment we are becoming a more diverse country, we are steering children and teens into increasingly segregated schools.

The changes the next millennium brings at the very least surpass and quite possibly will shatter our current understanding of race, ethnicity, culture and community. The real test of our strength will be how willing we are to go beyond the narrowness of our expectations, seek knowledge about the lives of those around us—and move forward with eagerness, not fear.

Racial "Diversity" Is Racism

by Peter Schwartz

About the author: *Peter Schwartz is chair of the board of directors at the Ayn Rand Institute in Irvine, California.*

Editor's Note: This article was written about the impending June 2003 Supreme Court decision in Grutter v. Bollinger.

President [George W.] Bush faces an ideal opportunity to take a principled position on the issue of racial "diversity." As his administration ponders whether to support the legal challenge, now before the Supreme Court, to the University of Michigan's affirmative action policies, he should go further and raise a *moral* challenge to the entire notion of "diversity." Instead of timidly wavering on this question, in fear of being smeared by Democrats as racist, President Bush should rise to the occasion by categorically repudiating racism—and condemning "diversity" as its worst manifestation.

It is now widely accepted that "diversity" is an appropriate goal for society. But what does this dictum actually mean? Racial integration is a valid objective, but that is something very different from what the advocates of "diversity" seek. They claim that we must divide people by race, in order to be exposed to new perspectives on life. We supposedly gain "enrichment from the differences in viewpoint of minorities," as the *MIT Faculty Newsletter* puts it. Admissions should be based on race, the University of Michigan's vice president says, because "learning in a diverse environment benefits all students, minority and majority alike."

The Essence of Racism

These circumlocutions translate simply into this: one's race determines the content of one's mind. They imply that people have worthwhile views to express because of their ethnicity, and that "diversity" enables us to encounter "black ideas," "Hispanic ideas," etc. What could be more repulsively racist than that? This is exactly the premise held by the South's slave-owners and by the Nazis' Storm Troopers. They too believed that an individual's thoughts and actions are determined by his racial heritage.

Whether a given race receives special rewards or special punishments is immaterial. The essence of racism is the idea that the individual is meaningless and that membership in the collective—the race—is the source of his identity and value. To the racist, the individual's moral and intellectual character is the product not of his own choices, but of the genes he shares with all others of his race. To the racist, the particular members of a given race are interchangeable.

"Racial 'diversity' is a doctrine that splits people into ethnic tribes, which then battle one another for special favors."

The advocates of "diversity" similarly believe that colleges must admit not individuals, but "representatives" of various races. They believe that those representatives have certain ideas innately imprinted on their minds, and that giving preferences to minority races creates a "diversity" of viewpoints on campus. They have the quota-mentality, which holds that in judging someone, the salient fact is the racial collective to which he belongs.

This philosophy is why racial division is *growing* at our colleges. The segregated dormitories, the segregated cafeterias, the segregated fraternities—these all exist, not in spite of the commitment to "diversity," but because of it. The overriding message of "diversity," transmitted by the policies of a school's administration and by the teachings of a school's professors, is that the individual is defined by his race. It is no surprise, then, that many students associate only with members of their own race and regard others as belonging to alien tribes.

The Importance of Individualism

If racism is to be rejected, it is the premise of individualism, including individual free will, that must be upheld. There is no way to bring about racial integration except by completely disregarding color. There is no benefit in being exposed to the thoughts of a black person as opposed to a white person; there is a benefit only in interacting with individuals, of *any* race, who have rational viewpoints to offer.

"Diversity," in any realm, has no value in and of itself. Investors can be urged to diversify their holdings—but for the sake of minimizing their financial risk, not for the sake of "diversity" as such. To maintain that "diversity" per se is desirable—that "too much" of one thing is objectionable—is ludicrous. Do brown-eyed students need to be "diversified" with green-eyed ones? Does one's unimpaired health need to be "diversified" with bouts of illness? Or knowledge with ignorance?

The value of a racially integrated student body or work force lies entirely in the individualism this implies—i.e., in the fact that the students or workers were chosen objectively, with skin color ignored in favor of the standard of individual merit. But that is *not* what the advocates of "diversity" want. They sneer at the principle of "color-blindness." They want decisions on college or job applicants to be made exactly as the vilest of racists make them: by bloodline. They insist that whatever is a result of your own choices—your ideas, your character, your accomplishments—is to be dismissed, while that which is outside your control—the accident of skin color—is to define your life. Their fundamental goal is to "diversify"—and thus to undercut—the standard of individual achievement with the non-standard of race.

Racial "diversity" is a doctrine that splits people into ethnic tribes, which then battle one another for special favors. If President Bush is eager to demonstrate his disagreement with the racist views of a Strom Thurmond [the former Republican senator of South Carolina] let him stand up and denounce all forms of racism—particularly, the one that underlies "diversity."

Activists Fighting Racism Should Engage in Nonviolent Revolution

by Grace Lee Boggs

About the author: *Grace Lee Boggs is an activist, writer, and speaker whose political involvement encompasses the labor, civil rights, women's liberation, and environmental justice movements in the United States.*

In the 1960s I didn't pay much attention to Martin Luther King, Jr. My own social-change activities unfolded in the inner city of Detroit [Michigan]. So I identified more with Malcolm [X] than with Martin. Like most Black Power activists, I tended to view King's notions of nonviolence and "the beloved community" as somewhat naive and sentimental.

Nor was I involved in the fifteen-year campaign that was launched in 1968 by Detroit's own Congressman John Conyers to declare King's birthday a national holiday. While many progressives rallied to the cause, I held back, concerned that it would turn King into an icon, obscure the role of grass-roots activists, and reinforce the tendency to rely on charismatic leaders.

[More than] thirty-five years have passed since King was killed—decades during which many of us have continued to struggle to free our communities of crime, violence, and economic devastation. In the wake of the urban rebellions of the late 1960s, the violence and fear have only escalated. In the [more than] twenty years since Ronald Reagan signed into law the King holiday, we seem to have drifted further from anything resembling a beloved community in this nation.

Thinking back over these years, I can't help wondering: Might events have taken a different path if we had found a way to infuse our struggle for Black Power with King's philosophy and ideology of nonviolence? Is it possible that our relationships with one another today, not only inter- but intra-racially, would be more respectful and harmonious if we had discovered how to blend

Malcolm's militancy with King's beloved community?

Could such a symbiosis have a revolutionary power beyond our wildest dreams? And, I dare to wonder, is such a revolutionary power available to us today?

The Weakness of Marx and Lenin

I cut my own activist teeth, as did many of my generation, on the revolutionary theories of Marx and Lenin. Their ideas and strategies were developed during the industrial era, when the prevailing concern of social-change activists was to extend our material powers. People's lives were determined by economic necessities—hence our strategies for radical change centered on the economic arena. The goal was to help workers understand that they were victims of the economic system, and that the only solution was to get rid of it. We struggled for political power as a way to abolish the unjust economic system. That is still the revolutionary scenario for most radicals, including African Americans and other persons of color.

> *"We can no longer define struggle simply in terms of us versus them, victims versus villains, good versus evil."*

One of the weaknesses of such a revolutionary vision is its failure to recognize the great divide created by the dropping of the atom bombs that ended World War II. The splitting of the atom brought human beings face to face with the reality that we had expanded our material powers to the point where we could destroy our planet. No longer could we afford to act as if everything that happened to us was determined by external or economic circumstances.

This crucial juncture in human evolution required (and requires) a profound change in theories of revolutionary struggle. No longer can we view radical social change as a D-day replacement of one set of rulers with another. We can no longer define struggle simply in terms of us versus them, victims versus villains, good versus evil. We can no longer focus only on transferring power from the top to the bottom. Henceforth, we need to grasp a process of transformation that includes both ourselves and our institutions, that fuses politics with ethics, that operates according to a consciously created integrity of ends and means.

That is why, as I have been reading and re-reading King's speeches and writings from the last two years of his life, it has become increasingly clear to me that King's social ministry and prophetic vision are now the indispensable starting point for twenty-first-century revolutionaries.

A Successful Struggle Against Racism

The civil rights movement, launched by the Montgomery Bus Boycott in 1955, was the first struggle by an oppressed people in Western society from this new post-atomic perspective. Tens of thousands of African Americans in Montgomery carried out a year-long nonviolent, disciplined, and ultimately successful struggle against racist structures. Before the eyes of the whole world, a people who had been treated as less than human struggled against their dehumanization not as angry victims or rebels but as new men and women, representative of a new more human society. They used methods that transformed themselves and increased the good rather than the evil in the world. By always bearing in mind that their goal was not only desegregation of the buses but the beloved community, they inspired the human-identity and ecological movements which over the last forty years have been creating a new civil society in the United States.

King's speeches and writings, produced in the heat of struggle, played a critical role in the success of Montgomery and later struggles. As a Black man living in the racist United States and as a philosopher, King was supremely conscious of the contradiction between our technological overdevelopment and our human underdevelopment—as he often put it, we have "guided missiles and misguided men."

King constantly pointed out to those in the freedom movement that their refusal to respond in kind to the violence and terrorism of their opponents was increasing their own strength and unity. He constantly reminded them and the world that their goal was not only the right to sit at the front of the bus or to vote, but to give birth to a new society based on more human values. In so doing, he not only empowered those on the frontlines, but in the process developed a new strategy for transforming a struggle for rights into a struggle that advances the humanity of everyone in the society and thereby brings the beloved community closer.

> *"A nonviolent revolution . . . [could] combine the struggle against racism with a struggle against poverty, militarism, and materialism."*

Redefining Basic Political Concepts

Essential to King's power as a revolutionary was his capacity, in the midst of specific struggles to redefine basic concepts of political philosophy and practice.

Take, for example, the concept of freedom. Most people in the United States think of freedom in terms of the individual—the right to "do your own thing." They also believe that the United States has the right and responsibility to spread and defend this concept of freedom around the world. King's experiences as an African American man in a racist society had taught him the limitations of this unhistorical understanding.

Freedom should not be viewed as an abstraction, he wrote. Nor can it be separated from necessity and responsibility. King urged us to look at freedom from the viewpoint of the whole person, viewing it as a process which involves our capacity to deliberate and weigh alternatives, to make choices, and then take responsibility for our decisions.

King proposed a similar enriching of our concept of love. Most people think of love only in terms of affection between lovers (eros) or friends (philia). Again, King's experiences of systemic racism had taught him that love of power goes hand in hand with domination and destruction of community. He developed a profoundly political concept of love (building on his theological understanding of love as agape) that is based on the willingness of the oppressed to go to any lengths to restore or create community. Practicing this concept of love empowers the oppressed to overcome fear and the oppressors to transcend hate.

Similarly, most people in the United States think of citizenship only in terms of loyalty to this country. King, whose ideas were developed in an era when liberation struggles were going on all over the world, recognized that the time had come for a more global concept of citizenship.

To become part of this world-wide fellowship, King believed that we must rapidly begin the shift from a "thing-oriented" society to a "person-oriented" society. "When machines and computers, profit motives, and property rights are considered more important than people," he warned, "the giant triplets of racism, materialism, and militarism are incapable of being conquered."

Viewing Martin Luther King, Jr. as a revolutionary is in sharp contrast to the "official" view of him as simply an advocate for the rights of African Americans within the current system. King was a revolutionary in the best sense of the word. In the wake of the youth rebellions in Northern cities, which required a more complex solution than visions of Black and White children marching hand in hand, King began to explore a new kind of revolution. He envisioned a nonviolent revolution that would challenge all the values and institutions of our society, and combine the struggle against racism with a struggle against poverty, militarism, and materialism. King sought to conceptualize a new system that would go beyond capitalism, which he said was too "I-centered, too individualistic," and communism, which he saw as "too collective, too statist."

Warning that material growth had been made an end in itself and that our scientific power had outrun our spiritual power, he refused to accept the dictatorship of High Tech, which diminishes people because it eliminates their sense of participation. King deplored the way that educators

> *"The life of an Afghani, Iraqi, Irani, North Korean, or Palestinian is as precious as the life of someone in the United States."*

were trying to instill middle-class values in Black youth, noting that "it was precisely when young Negroes threw off their middle-class values and put careers and wealth in a secondary role" that they made a historic social contribution. And he called for programs that would involve young people in direct actions "in our dying cities" that would be both self-transforming and structure-transforming.

King the revolutionary challenged not only political and economic systems, but our own internal understandings of ourselves and of the world. He called not just for new structures in power, but new kinds of power, rooted in democratic empowerment of all persons as bearing dignity and possibility. He sought out not simply new revolutionary ends, but revolutionary means that bore within themselves the character and quality of the ultimate goal, a beloved community of all persons. He articulated a dynamic and evolving process of revolution and transformation.

The Need for a Radical Revolution

We will never know what King might have done had he not been assassinated. What we do know is that, in the [more than] thirty-five years since his death, the "giant triplets" of racism, militarism, and materialism have become even more dehumanizing. Our communities have been turned into wastelands by economic disinvestment and the High-Tech juggernaut, and the youth in our de-industrialized cities have become increasingly desperate. Transnational corporations have spread their tentacles around the world, widening the gulf between rich and poor, robbing local communities of their sources of food, fuel, and local cultures. At the same time, U.S. military forces prop up compliant reactionary regimes, feeding resentment and breeding an international network of terrorists.

King's reasons for opposing the Vietnam War against communism in the 1960s can be applied almost verbatim to the current U.S. war against terrorism: "Poverty, insecurity, and injustice," he explained, "are the fertile soil in which the seed of communism grows." A positive revolution of values "is our best defense against communism. War is not the answer. . . . We must not engage in a negative anti-communism, but rather in a positive thrust for democracy."

Now is a ripe time to look anew at King's "radical revolution of values." Underneath the flag-waving that has been so visible since September 11, 2001, a great deal of soul-searching has been going on. Many people in the United States, faced with mortality on such an instant and colossal scale, have been reassessing their priorities and wondering how to make their lives more meaningful. In the process, some are beginning to recognize that spiritual values like compassion, generosity, and community are more important than material consumption.

As the [George W.] Bush administration continues to exploit popular fears to carry out its agenda of military buildup, cutbacks on social programs, and suppression of dissent, we need to tap into King's revolutionary spirit. We can find hope that increasing numbers of Americans will realize that the best way to insure our peace and security is not by warring on the "axis of evil" but through a radical revolution in our own values and practice. That revolution must include a concept of global citizenship in which the life of an Afghani, Iraqi, Irani, North Korean, or Palestinian is as precious as the life of someone in the United States.

We can gather as small groups, with our co-workers, neighbors, families, and church members, creating together a new language that describes the kind of new human beings and the kind of country we want to become. King's writings and speeches, especially "A Time to Break Silence" and *Where Do We Go From Here: Chaos or Community*, provide excellent material for small discussion groups.

We also need to engage in practical actions that help us transform ourselves and point the way towards the radical reconstruction of society that King advocated. Hopeful signs are popping up in cities and communities throughout the country. More than a hundred U.S. cities and four hundred more around the world have defied the Bush administration's abandonment of the Kyoto Treaty on global warming by devising local initiatives to meet the treaty's goals.

Numerous local groups are organizing programs to reduce our dependence on global capitalism by creating more self-reliant economies, including urban agriculture programs and local currencies like the Ithaca dollar. We need experiments in alternative education for our young people, like Detroit Summer and KIDS (Kids Involved in Direct Service), which are pioneering self-transforming and structure-transforming community-building programs, especially in our schools from K-12. We need more grassroots democratic institutions that stress participatory and decentralized citizen participation in all aspects of our community life.

We also need King's wisdom in re-envisioning our movements for social change. (I like to think, that based on the ideas that he was exploring in the last two years of his life. King would have been at the Battle of Seattle in November, 1999, and participating in the ensuing anti-globalization movement.) Following King's lead, we need movement-builders who, confident of their own humanity, are able to recognize the humanity in others, including their opponents, and therefore the potential within them for redemption. We need movement-builders who choose nonviolent struggle as a way of restoring community rather than increasing hate, fear, and bitterness. We need movement-builders who go beyond slogans and create programs of struggle that transform and empower participants—such as the Montgomery Bus Boycott's creation of an alternative self-reliant transportation system. We need movement-builders who recognize the need for two-sided transformation, both of ourselves and of our institutions, and who ensure that the methods we use in our struggles are transforming ourselves as well as our opponents toward a deeper, truer humanity.

> *"The survival of our planet and the restoration of our humanity require a great sea change in our ecological, economic, political, and spiritual values."*

These are tough and uncertain times. We need a vision that will do for our time what the beloved community did for King's. We need a vision that recognizes that we are at one of the great turning points in human history when the survival of our planet and the restoration of our humanity require a great sea change in our ecological, economic, political, and spiritual values.

Organizations to Contact

The editors have compiled the following list of organizations concerned with the issues debated in this book. The descriptions are derived from materials provided by the organizations. All have publications or information available for interested readers. The list was compiled on the date of publication of the present volume; the information provided here may change. Be aware that many organizations take several weeks or longer to respond to inquiries, so allow as much time as possible.

American-Arab Anti-Discrimination Committee (ADC)
4201 Connecticut Ave., Washington, DC 20008
(202) 244-2990 • fax: (202) 244-3196
e-mail: adc@adc.org • website: www.adc.org

ADC is a nonsectarian, nonpartisan civil rights organization dedicated to combating discrimination against people of Arab heritage and promoting intercultural awareness. It works to protect Arab American rights through a national network of chapters. The committee publishes the newsletter *ADC Times* ten times a year as well as an annual special report summarizing incidents of hate crimes, discrimination, and defamation against Arab Americans.

American Civil Liberties Union (ACLU)
125 Broad St., 18th Fl., New York, NY 10004
(212) 549-2585
website: www.aclu.org

The ACLU is a national organization that works to defend Americans' civil rights as guaranteed by the U.S. Constitution. The ACLU publishes and distributes policy statements, pamphlets, and the semiannual newsletter *Civil Liberties Alert*.

American Immigration Control Foundation (AIC)
PO Box 525, Monterey, VA 24465
(540) 468-2022 • fax: (540) 468-2024
e-mail: aicfndn@cfw.com • website: www.aicfoundation.com

The AIC Foundation is an independent research and education organization that believes massive immigration, especially illegal immigration, is harming America. It calls for an end to illegal immigration and for stricter controls on legal immigration. The foundation publishes several pamphlets, monographs, and booklets, including Joseph L. Daleiden's *Selling Our Birthright* and Lawrence Auster's *Huddled Cliches*.

Amnesty International (AI)
322 Eighth Ave., New York, NY 10004-2400
(212) 807-8400 • (800) AMNESTY (266-3789) • fax: (212) 627-1451
website: www.amnesty-usa.org

Founded in 1961, AI is a grassroots activist organization that aims to free all nonviolent people who have been imprisoned because of their beliefs, ethnic origin, sex, color, or language. The *Amnesty International Report* is published annually, and other reports are available online and by mail.

Cato Institute
1000 Massachusetts Ave. NW, Washington, DC 20001-5403
(202) 842-0200 • fax: (202) 842-3490
e-mail: cato@cato.org • website: www.cato.org

The Cato Institute is a libertarian public policy research foundation dedicated to limiting the role of government and protecting individual liberties. It researches claims of discrimination and opposes affirmative action. The institute offers numerous publications, including the *Cato Journal*, the bimonthly newsletter *Cato Policy Report*, and the quarterly magazine *Regulation.*

Center for the Study of Popular Culture
PO Box 67398, Los Angeles, CA 90067
(310) 843-3699 • fax: (310) 843-3692
e-mail: info@cspc.org • website: www.cspc.org

This educational center was started by commentators David Horowitz and Peter Collier, whose intellectual development evolved from support for the New Left in the 1960s to the forefront of today's conservatism. The center offers legal assistance and addresses many topics, including political correctness, multiculturalism, and discrimination. Its Individual Rights Foundation provides legal assistance to citizens challenging affirmative action. The center also publishes the online *FrontPage* magazine.

Center for the Study of White American Culture
245 W. 4th Ave., Roselle, NJ 07203
(908) 241-5439
e-mail: contact@euroamerican.org • website: www.euroamerican.org

The center is a multiracial organization that supports cultural exploration and self-discovery among white Americans. It also encourages dialogue among all racial and cultural groups concerning the role of white American culture in the larger American society. It publishes the Whiteness Papers series, including "Decentering Whiteness" and "White Men and the Denial of Racism."

Citizens' Commission on Civil Rights (CCCR)
2000 M St. NW, Suite 400, Washington, DC 20036
(202) 659-5565 • fax: (202) 223-5302
e-mail: citizens@cccr.org • website: www.cccr.org

CCCR monitors the federal government's enforcement of antidiscrimination laws and promotes equal opportunity for all. It publishes reports on affirmative action and desegregation as well as the book *One Nation Indivisible: The Civil Rights Challenge for the 1990s.*

Commission for Racial Justice (CRJ)
700 Prospect Ave., Cleveland, OH 44115-1110
(216) 736-2100 • fax: (216) 736-2171

CRJ was formed in 1963 by the United Church of Christ in response to racial tensions gripping the nation at that time. Its goal is a peaceful, dignified society where all men and women are equal. CRJ publishes various documents and books, such as *Racism and the Pursuit of Racial Justice* and *A National Symposium on Race and Housing in the United States: Challenges for the 21st Century.*

Heritage Foundation
214 Massachusetts Ave. NE, Washington, DC 20002-4999
(202) 546-4400 • fax: (202) 546-8328
e-mail: info@heritage.org • website: www.heritage.org

The Heritage Foundation is a public policy research institute that advocates limited government and the free market system. It opposes affirmative action and believes the private sector, not government, should be relied upon to ease social problems and improve the status of minorities. The foundation publishes the bimonthly journal *Policy Review* as well as hundreds of monographs, books, and papers on public policy issues.

Hispanic Policy Development Project (HPDP)
1001 Connecticut Ave. NW, Suite 901, Washington, DC 20036
(202) 822-8414 • fax: (202) 822-9120

HPDP encourages the analysis of public policies affecting Hispanics in the United States, particularly the education, training, and employment of Hispanic youth. It publishes a number of books and pamphlets, including *Together Is Better: Building Strong Partnerships Between Schools and Hispanic Parents.*

National Association for the Advancement of Colored People (NAACP)
4805 Mt. Hope Dr., Baltimore, MD 21215-3297
(410) 358-8900 • fax: (410) 486-9257
website: www.naacp.org

The NAACP is the oldest and largest civil rights organization in the United States. Its principal objective is to ensure the political, educational, social, and economic equality of minorities. It publishes the magazine *Crisis* ten times a year as well as a variety of newsletters, books, and pamphlets.

National Network for Immigrant and Refugee Rights (NNIRR)
310 Eighth St., Suite 307, Oakland, CA 94607
(510) 465-1984 • fax: (510) 465-1885
e-mail: nnirr@igc.apc.org • website: www.nnirr.org

The network includes community, church, labor, and legal groups committed to the cause of equal rights for all immigrants. These groups work to end discrimination and unfair treatment of illegal immigrants and refugees. It publishes a monthly newsletter, *Network News.*

National Urban League
120 Wall St., 8th Fl., New York, NY 10005
(212) 558-5300 • fax: (212) 344-5332
website: www.nul.org

A community service agency, the National Urban League aims to eliminate institutional racism in the United States. It also provides services for minorities who experience discrimination in employment, housing, welfare, and other areas. It publishes the report *The Price: A Study of the Costs of Racism in America* and the annual *State of Black America.*

Poverty and Race Research Action Council (PRRAC)
3000 Connecticut Ave. NW, Suite 200, Washington, DC 20008
(202) 387-9887 • fax: (202) 387-0764
e-mail: info@prrac.org

The Poverty and Race Research Action Council is a nonpartisan, national, not-for-profit organization convened by major civil rights, civil liberties, and anti-poverty groups. PRRAC's purpose is to link social science research to advocacy work in order to successfully address problems at the intersection of race and poverty. Its bimonthly publication, *Poverty and Race*, often includes articles on race- and income-based inequities in the United States.

The Prejudice Institute
Stephens Hall Annex, TSU, Towson, MD 21204-7097
(410) 830-2435 • fax: (410) 830-2455

The Prejudice Institute is a national research center concerned with violence and intimidation motivated by prejudice. It conducts research, supplies information on model programs and legislation, and provides education and training to combat prejudicial violence. The Prejudice Institute publishes research reports, bibliographies, and the quarterly newsletter *Forum.*

Sojourners
2401 15th St. NW, Washington, DC 20009
(202) 328-8842 • (800) 714-7474 • fax: (202) 328-8757
e-mail: sojourners@sojourners.com • website: www.sojourners.com

Sojourners is an ecumenical Christian organization committed to racial justice and reconciliation between the races. It publishes *America's Original Sin: A Study and Guide on White Racism* as well as the monthly *Sojourners* magazine.

United States Commission on Civil Rights
624 Ninth St. NW, Suite 500, Washington, DC 20425
(202) 376-7533 • fax: (202) 376-8128

A fact-finding body, the commission reports directly to Congress and the president on the effectiveness of equal opportunity laws and programs. A catalog of its numerous publications can be obtained from its Publication Management Division.

Bibliography

Books

Annie S. Barnes	*Everyday Racism: A Book for All Americans.* Naperville, IL: Sourcebooks, 2000.
Bob Blauner	*Still the Big News: Racial Oppression in America.* Philadelphia: Temple University Press, 2001.
Lawrence Blum	*"I'm Not a Racist, But . . .": The Moral Quandary of Race.* Ithaca, NY: Cornell University Press, 2002.
William G. Bowen and Derek Curtis Bok	*The Shape of the River: Long-Term Consequences of Considering Race in College and University Admissions.* Princeton, NJ: Princeton University Press, 1998.
David Brook	*The World Conference Against Racism: The Adoption and Repeal of the Z=R Resolution and the Implications for U.N. Reform.* Wayne, NJ: Center for U.N. Reform Education, 2001.
Michael K. Brown	*Whitewashing Race: The Myth of a Color-Blind Society.* Berkeley: University of California Press, 2003.
Stephen M. Cahn	*Affirmative Action Debate*, 2nd edition. New York: Routledge, 2002.
David Mark Chalmers	*Backfire: How the Ku Klux Klan Helped the Civil Rights Movement.* Lanham, MD: Rowman & Littlefield, 2003.
Mary Jane Collier	*Building Intercultural Alliances.* Thousand Oaks, CA: Sage, 2002.
Dalton Conley	*Honky.* New York: Vintage, 2001.
Ward Connerly	*Creating Equal: My Fight Against Racial Preference.* San Francisco: Encounter Books, 2000.
Joe R. Feagin	*Racist America: Roots, Current Realities, and Future Reparations.* New York: Routledge, 2000.
Joseph L. Graves Jr.	*The Emperor's New Clothes: Biological Theories of Race at the Millennium.* Piscataway, NJ: Rutgers University Press, 2003.
Andrea Guerrero	*Silence at Boalt Hall: The Dismantling of Affirmative Action.* Berkeley: University of California Press, 2002.

Bibliography

David Horowitz — *Uncivil Wars: The Controversy over Reparations for Slavery.* San Francisco: Encounter Books, 2003.

Randall Kennedy — *Nigger: The Strange Career of a Troublesome Word.* New York: Knopf, 2003.

Paul Kivel and Howard Zinn — *Uprooting Racism: How White People Can Work for Racial Justice.* Gabriola Island, BC: New Society, 2002.

Elisabeth Lasch-Quinn — *Race Experts: How Racial Etiquette, Sensitivity Training, and New Age Therapy Hijacked the Civil Rights Revolution.* New York: W.W. Norton, 2001.

Manning Marable — *The Great Wells of Democracy: The Meaning of Race in American Life.* New York: Basic Civitas Books, 2002.

Deborah Mathis — *Yet a Stranger: Why Black Americans Still Don't Feel at Home.* New York: Warner Books, 2003.

Stephen Grant Meyer — *As Long As They Don't Move Next Door: Segregation and Racial Conflict in American Neighborhoods.* New York: Rowman & Littlefield, 2000.

Gary Orfield and Michal Kurlaender — *Diversity Challenged: Evidence on the Impact of Affirmative Action.* Cambridge, MA: Harvard Education Publishing Group, 2001.

Kevin Reilly, Stephen Kaufman, and Angela Bodino, eds. — *Racism: A Global Reader.* Armonk, NY: M.E. Sharpe, 2002.

Jo Ann Ooiman Robinson — *Affirmative Action: A Documentary History.* Westport, CT: Greenwood, 2001.

Paula S. Rothenberg, ed. — *White Privilege: A Reader.* New York: Worth Publications, 2001.

Philip F. Rubio — *A History of Affirmative Action: 1619–2000.* Jackson: University Press of Mississippi, 2001.

Pat Shipman — *The Evolution of Racism.* Cambridge, MA: Harvard University Press, 2002.

Jim Sleeper — *Liberal Racism: How Fixating on Race Subverts the American Dream.* 2nd Edition. Lanham, MD: Rowman & Littlefield, 2002.

Stephen Steinberg — *Turning Back: The Retreat from Racial Justice in American Thought and Policy.* Boston: Beacon Press, 2001.

Leonard Steinhorn and Barbara Diggs-Brown — *By the Color of Our Skin: The Illusion of Integration and the Reality of Race.* New York: Penguin, 1999.

Stephan Thernstrom and Abigail Thernstrom — *America in Black and White: One Nation, Indivisible.* New York: Simon and Schuster, 1997.

Becky Thompson — *A Promise and a Way of Life: White Antiracist Activism.* Minneapolis: University of Minnesota Press, 2001.

| Cooper Thompson, Emmett Robert Shaefer, and Harry Brod | *Just Living: White Men Challenging Racism.* Durham, NC: Duke University Press, 2003. |
| Leon Wynter | *American Skin: Pop Culture, Big Business, and the End of White America.* New York: Crown, 2002. |

Periodicals

Ricardo Alonso-Zalvidar	"Latino Survey Shows Optimism About Assimilation," *Los Angeles Times*, December 18, 2002.
Kirsten Betsworth and Molly M. Ginty	"Legacy of Hate: After Seven Long Years, I Finally Left My Husband and His Racist White Pride Group," *Good Housekeeping*, July 2001.
Nick Bonokoski	"The New Racism," *Briarpatch*, May 2002.
Graham Boyd	"The Drug War Is the New Jim Crow," *NACLA Report on the Americas*, July 2001.
Fidel Castro	"The Roots of International Racism," *Monthly Review*, December 2001.
Trevor W. Coleman	"Race Matters," *Crisis*, November/December 2002.
Ward Connerly	"Laying Down the Burden of Race," *American Enterprise*, June 2000.
Ellis Cose	"What's White, Anyway?" *Newsweek*, September 18, 2000.
Shikha Dalmia	"The Diversity Defense," *Weekly Standard*, March 26, 2001.
David Brion Davis	"Jews, Blacks, and the Roots of Racism," *Midstream*, December 2001.
Ronald Dworkin	"Race and the Uses of Law," *New York Times*, April 13, 2001.
Richard Estrada	"Hispanics and the Question of Color," *San Diego Union-Tribune*, October 6, 1999.
Gabriel Fawcett	"Teaching History and the German Right," *History Today*, February 2001.
Ethan Flad	"Reparations Is Not About Money," *Witness*, December 2002.
Lani Guinier and Gerald Torres	"The Miner's Canary: The Problems of People of Color Show What's Wrong with American Democracy," *Nation*, February 18, 2002.
George Henderson	"Race in America," *National Forum*, Spring 2000.
Issues and Controversies On File	"Slavery Reparations," December 15, 2000.
Jesse L. Jackson Sr.	"Race and Racism in America," *National Forum*, Spring 2000.
Tamar Jacoby	"Beyond Busing," *Wall Street Journal*, July 21, 1999.

Bibliography

Clara Sue Kidwell, Homer Noley, and George E. Tinker   "A Fragile Miracle: Defying Five Hundred Years of Conquest, Native People Continue to Survive . . ." *Other Side*, November/December 2001.

Alan Charles Kors   "Thought Reform 101," *Reason*, March 2000.

Joyce A. Ladner   "A New Civil Rights Agenda," *Brookings Review*, Spring 2000.

Michael Lind   "The Diversity Scam," *New Leader*, July 2000.

Heather MacDonald   "What Looks Like Profiling Might Just Be Good Policing," *Los Angeles Times*, January 19, 2003.

Timothy W. Maier   "Army of Bias?" *Insight*, September 24, 2001.

Rania Masri   "Combating Racism: Only Together—With Our Arms Locked," *International Socialist Review*, August/September 2001.

John McWhorter   "We're Not Ready to Think Outside the Box on Race," *Wall Street Journal*, March 28, 2002.

Peter Noel   "Portraits in Racial Profiling," *Village Voice*, March 21, 2000.

Gary Orfield   "Schools More Separate: Consequences of a Decade of Resegregation," *Rethinking Schools*, Fall 2001.

Orlando Patterson   "Race by the Numbers," *New York Times*, May 8, 2001.

Adolph L. Reed Jr.   "The Case Against Reparations," *Progressive*, December 2000.

Camille Mojica Rey   "Making Room for Diversity Makes Sense," *Science*, August 31, 2001.

Jason L. Riley   "The 'Diversity' Defense," *Commentary*, April 2001.

John O'Neal Roach   "Discriminating Positively: Preferential Acceptance of Minorities May Be Good for Society," *Western Journal of Medicine*, October 2001.

Jeffrey Rosen   "Without Merit—For Race in Class," *New Republic*, May 14, 2001.

Kevin Sack with Janet Elder   "Poll Finds Optimistic Outlook But Enduring Racial Division," *New York Times*, July 11, 2000.

Roy H. Saigo   "Why Asian-Americans Deserve Better than We Get," *San Diego Union-Tribune*, October 27, 1999.

Lance Selfa   "Slavery and the Origins of Racism," *International Socialist Review*, November/December 2002.

Michael E. Sherifis   "A Vast, Afflicted Landscape," *UN Chronicle*, June/August 2001.

Shelby Steele   "Making Colorblindness a Reality," *Wall Street Journal*, March 29, 2002.

Linda Villarosa   "Beyond Black and White in Biology and Medicine," *New York Times*, January 1, 2002.

Dale Weiss	"Confronting White Privilege," *Rethinking Schools*, Summer 2002.
Howard Winant	"Race in the Twenty-First Century," *Tikkun*, January/February 2002.
Raymond A. Winbush	"Back to the Future: Campus Racism in the 21st Century," *Black Collegian*, October 2001.
G. Pascal Zachary	"A Mixed Future," *Wall Street Journal*, January 1, 2000.
Mortimer B. Zuckerman	"A Shameful Contagion," *U.S. News & World Report*, October 7, 2002.

Index

Index